W9-BJI-860

# Touring the
# San Francisco
# Bay Area
## by Bicycle

By Peter Powers

Edited by Melissa Carlson

Cover photo of the Golden Gate Bridge
by Ed Cooper Photo

Inset photo of Pam Fomalont by Ron Fomalont

First Edition

**TERRAGRAPHICS**

Eugene, Oregon

# Touring the
# San Francisco
# Bay Area
## by Bicycle

For Claire,
whose legs are still too short to reach the
pedals.

## Acknowledgements

The routes that are detailed in this book were
suggested by a group of women and men who are
very familiar with the ups and downs of cycling in
the Bay Area. Our thanks to Ken Aslin, Dan Belick,
Liz Coyle, Mick Coyle, Kirsten Goettler, David Goettler, James Hill, Mike Jacoubowski, Kris Knudsen,
Al Knudsen, and Matt Sharp for their help.

©1990 by Peter Powers and Renée Travis. All rights
reserved, which includes the right to reproduce this
book or portions thereof in any form whatsoever
except as provided by the U.S. Copyright Law.

For information contact the author at
P.O. Box 1025, Eugene, OR USA 97440

First edition, first printing.
Published by Terragraphics
P.O. Box 1025, Eugene, OR 97440

Printed in the United States of America

**ISBN 0-944376-05-3**

# Contents

                                              (cont.)

# Introduction

**I**n an area so involved with motorized transport, it is surprising how many great opportunities the Bay Area offers for enjoying a day on your bike. The range of cycling experiences is extensive - from one lane country roads in areas far removed from the intensity of the city, to bike lanes that share a four lane highway with all kinds of moving vehicles. The contributors of routes for this book, all avid Bay Area cyclists, have explored most of these opportunities. Several are in the bicycle retailing business and are excellent sources of information about rides and equipment.

Outside the city of San Francisco, there are three major regions around the Bay which have a wide variety of topography, climate and vegetation. North of San Francisco, Marin County exemplifies this diversity. In the southern part of the county, closer to San Francisco, the routes - even when they traverse the open lands of the Golden Gate National Recreation Area and Mt. Tamalpais State Park - tend to be busy, especially on weekends. Further north you can find true country riding on narrow roads that wind through miles of rural countryside. Climbing the hills of the coast range offers both a physical challenge and spectacular views.

The East Bay region, especially once you have crossed over the hills behind Berkeley and Oakland, also presents some wide open areas, but with a drier feel to them. The East Bay Regional Park District maintains several large Regional Parks, Preserves and Wildernesses that provide places to rest, picnic, swim, hike and try your hand at off road cycling. Over here the wind can become as much a factor in testing you physically as can a long hill.

To the south of San Francisco, the Peninsula region extends down to Santa Cruz and is dominated by the hills of the coast range. Bike routes in this area tend to wander through the foothills, cross over, or follow along the spine of these mountains.

Steep ascents and descents are characteristic of these rides and call for extra caution. As with Marin County to the north, there can be dramatic changes in the weather on east and west sides of the range, and being prepared means having an extra layer of clothing along for the ride.

The focus of this book is its set of maps. They are as complete as they are unique. Touring, whether by foot or bicycle, throws us into an intimate relationship with the topography of a chosen route. Hills can become mountains and grades can seem to go on forever when you are under your own power. What looks like a winding country road on a typical map may actually be a series of switchbacks that climbs up and over yet another ridge separating you from your destination! The 3D maps developed for this book provide you with a true representation of the landscape. The mileage log and route profile complete the picture of the ride ahead. They won't make it any easier to grind up and over those hills, but they will definitely take some of the unknown, and worry, out of your trip.

Along with the maps in this book, you'll find some general information pertinent to bicycle touring in this area. Other books cover any one of these topics in great detail. It is especially important that you become informed about fitness, with an emphasis on developing a good understanding of your capabilities and needs. Touring should be fun and fulfilling - not an unpleasant chore!

This book was designed to be taken with you as you venture around urban areas and into the countryside. The compact size is manageable for pocket or pack, and the layout will facilitate the navigation of each route.

The last section of the book has a reader response form that you are encouraged to fill out and mail to the author. Since these maps are new in concept and application, your comments will be very useful in improving and modifying future editions of this book. They will also help us compile books of other areas and of different activities.

Happy touring!

Pete Powers

# Using this book

**T**he addition of the third dimension to the maps in this book sets them apart from other recreation maps. The computer generated view of the earth's surface provides valuable and clear information about the topography of an area you are planning to tour on bicycle. These 3D views accurately portray the nature of the landscape and the road system that covers it. Combined with the road map, route profile, route log and description, they provide you with a complete picture of many of the routes to explore in this region.

## The area mapped

A good portion of the area around the San Francisco Bay is covered by the maps in this book. The 34 routes that are profiled in the 17 map sets are all loops that reach from Petaluma to Santa Cruz and as far east as Concord. They include a wide range of lengths and topography, providing the opportunity for everyone to pick a route for their ability and interest.

## About the maps

While each individual map covers only a portion of the Bay Area, the entire book presents you with a picture of the whole region. Each map highlights one or two ways to navigate around a specific area. Use of the profile to evaluate hilliness and length of a route allows you to estimate how long it will take to complete it. The 3D map and road map provide the information you need to pick an alternate route, or to shorten the one profiled.

The road maps are all oriented with north straight up, while the 3D maps rotate north to get the most complete view of the routes. Be aware that the scale of each map varies depending on the extent of the area being displayed.

*(continued on page 12)*

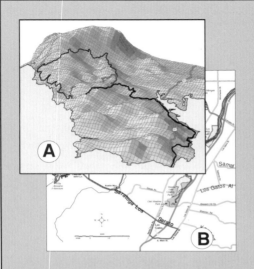

## Map elements

**A** **3D map.** This map shows the topography of the area and highlights the selected route. It includes most of the roads and features shown on the road map, including the area's alternate bike routes.

**B** **Road map.** This is the traditional "planimetric" map showing the route and significant roads, towns, water, geographic features, and map symbols. The mileposts along the route, as well as "direction of travel" arrows, are shown.

**C** **Route profile.** This provides a cross-sectional view of each route. Elevation lines are labeled on both left and right sides, and mileage references are indicated along the bottom. Identifiable features are located along the route to help you see where you are.

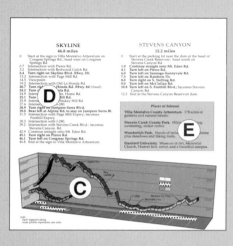

**D** **Route log.** This is a complete set of directions for navigating through each route. It is especially useful in weaving your way through congested urban areas.

**E** **Places of interest**. These are just some of the attractions along or near the highlighted routes.

**Index map.** *(Title page of map set).* This small map locates the area covered by the larger maps on the following pages.

**Calorie counter.** *(End page of map set).* This shows estimates for calories burned for cycling the mapped routes. Total calories expended over the entire loop are estimated for various average cycling speeds, and doesn't take hills into account.

The route profiles are all displayed at the same scale so you can easily compare them to each other. Don't be alarmed that some of them look more like a trip across the Sierra Nevada mountains than Bay Area topography - the vertical scale is exaggerated so that more of the "up and down" detail shows. Your first couple of rides will let your eyes and legs reach an understanding of how steep those hills really are!

## Liability disclaimer

The goal of this publication from Terragraphics is to provide the most accurate and useful maps possible for Bay Area cyclists. The 'alternate routes' displayed on these maps were compiled from a variety of sources, including city, county and state agencies and area cyclists. Along with the profiled routes, they are identified as being better suited for bicycle travel for safety, aesthetic or convenience reasons. Terragraphics assumes no liability for bicyclists travelling on these suggested routes. The maps are intended to aid in the selection of routes, but do not guarantee safety upon these roads. As with cycling on any road or trail, the cyclist assumes a risk while riding these suggested routes.

# Resources

**O**ne of the attractive aspects of cycling as a participant sport is the convenience of being able to engage in it at will, be it alone or with company. However, at times you may wish for more information, or for more structure, or more diversity for your bike touring. The maps in this book provide you with enough information to plan and enjoy many different rides. It is always advisable to carry along a map that has a complete inventory of streets, especially in the more urban areas. If deciding where to go on your next ride calls for more information for exploring unfamiliar territory, some of the following resources may help you with your planning. This is definitely not a comprehensive list, and one of the best sources of information is always the folks at a bike shop in the area where you plan to cycle.

## Maps

1. *Specific to bicycling.*

    **San Francisco Biking/Walking Guide**. Rufus Graphics.

    **Bicycle Commute Map of the East Bay.** East Bay Bicycle Coalition, Oakland.

    **Bikeways Santa Clara County.** Santa Clara County Transportation Agency, Milpitas.

    **Santa Cruz County Bikeways.** Santa Cruz Co. Transportation Commission, Santa Cruz.

    **Trails of the East Bay Hills** and **Trails of Mt. Tamalpais.** (Off road cycling). Olmstead Bros. Map Co., Berkeley.

2. *General street maps.*

    **Thomas Bros. Maps** for each county.

    **Rand McNally** county and city maps.

    **California State Automobile Association** county maps (members only).

3. *Topographic maps.*
 **USGS and BLM topographic maps.** U.S. Dept. of the Interior, San Francisco.

## Books
1. **Marin County Bike Trails.** Phyllis Neumann. Penngrove Publications.
2. **Marin Bike Paths.** Tacy Dunham.
3. **Roads to Ride** (Alameda, Contra Costa and Marin counties). Grant Petersen. Heyday Books.
4. **Roads to Ride** (San Mateo, Santa Clara and Santa Cruz counties). Grant Petersen. Heyday Books.

## Magazines
1. **California Bicyclist** (Northern edition). San Francisco.

## Clubs and organizations
The following groups include recreation oriented, on road cycling in their activities. There are many more groups in the Bay Area that focus on off road riding, racing and training, touring, and advocating for bicycle issues. The "Pedaler's Guide" in California Cyclist (Northern edition) contains a complete listing of bicycle associated clubs and organizations in the Bay Area.

1. **Different Spokes.** Box 14711, SF 94114 (415)282-1647.
2. **The Fogtown Frenzy.** 1454 34th. Ave., SF 94122 (415)731-3644.
3. **Golden Gate Cyclists, AYH.** 425 Divisadero, Suite 306, SF 94117 (415)863-9939.
4. **Marin Cyclists.** Box 2611, San Rafael 94902 (415)759-1205.
5. **Sierra Club (Bicycling section).** 3632 Lawton #5, SF 94122 (415)665-7913.
6. **Cherry City Cyclists.** Box 1972, San Leandro 94577 (415)562-8776.
7. **The Cyclery Group.** Contra Costa County (415)930-7012.
8. **Grizzly Peak Cyclists.** Box 9308, Berkeley 94709 (415)655-4221.
9. **Oakland Yellowjackets.** Oakland (415)835-8763.
10. **Almaden Cycle Touring Club.** Box 7286, San Jose 95150 (408)338-2663.

11. **Coastside Cyclist.** 852 Buena Vista, Moss Beach 94038 (415)728-5848.
12. **Western Wheelers Bicycle Club, Inc**. Box 518, Palo Alto 94302.

# General information

Information about attractions, parks, historic areas, and recreation opportunities is available from the following sources. Bookstores and libraries also offer a wide range of books and guides to interesting destinations and activities in the Bay Area.

## City/county

Visitor information:
1. **San Francisco Convention and Visitors Bureau**. P.O. Box 6977, SF 94101
2. **Marin County Chamber of Commerce and Visitors Bureau.** 30 N. Pedro Rd., San Rafael 91903
3. **Berkeley Convention and Tourist Services.** 1834 University Ave., Berkeley 94703
4. **Oakland Convention and Visitors Bureau.** 1000 Broadway, Oakland 94607
5. **Walnut Creek Chamber of Commerce.** 1395 Civic Dr., Walnut Creek 94596
6. **San Mateo County Convention and Visitors Bureau.** 601 Gateway Blvd., South SF 94080
7. **Palo Alto Chamber of Commerce.** 2450 El Camino Real, Palo Alto 94306
8. **San Jose Chamber of Commerce.** One Paseo de San Antonio, San Jose 95150
9. **Redwood Empire Association.** (Visitors' Guide for San Francisco and Marin Counties). One Market Plaza, Spear Street Tower, Suite 1001, SF 94105

Parks and Recreation:
1. **Marin County Dept. of Parks and Recreation**. Civic Center Dr., San Rafael 94901
2. **San Francisco Recreation and Parks Dept.** McClaren Lodge, Golden Gate Park, SF 94117
3. **San Mateo Parks and Recreation Division.** 590 Hamilton St., Redwood City 94063
4. **Santa Clara County Parks Dept.** 298 Garden Hill Dr., Los Gatos 95030

## Regional

1. **East Bay Regional Park District**. 11500 Skyline Blvd., Oakland 94619

2. **Midpeninsula Regional Open Space District**.
   Old Mill Office Center, Bldg. C, Suite 135, 201
   San Antonio Circle, Mountain View  94040

*State*

1. **California Department of Parks and Recreation**. P.O. Box 2390, Sacramento  95811

*National*

1. **National Park Service.**  Fort Mason, Building
   201, SF 94123
2. **Golden Gate National Recreation Area.**  Headquarters: Fort Mason, Building 201, SF 94123

# Map Symbols

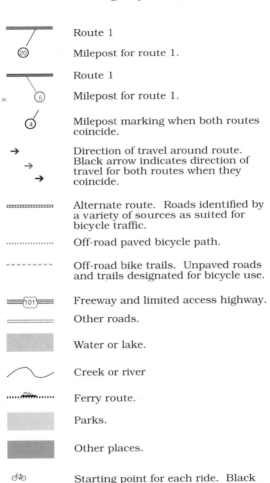

Route 1

Milepost for route 1.

Route 1

Milepost for route 1.

Milepost marking when both routes coincide.

Direction of travel around route. Black arrow indicates direction of travel for both routes when they coincide.

Alternate route. Roads identified by a variety of sources as suited for bicycle traffic.

Off-road paved bicycle path.

Off-road bike trails. Unpaved roads and trails designated for bicycle use.

Freeway and limited access highway.

Other roads.

Water or lake.

Creek or river

Ferry route.

Parks.

Other places.

Starting point for each ride. Black bicycle indicates a common starting point for both routes.

Olema          Small town or community.

**Berkeley**      Larger town or city.

# Map Scale

The scale of each map varies according to the amount of land covered. Refer to the scale bar to estimate distances on the street map. The 3D map is presented in perspective view - i.e. the scale gets smaller from front to back. The route profiles are displayed in a common scale in order to allow easier comparisons between all routes in the book.

# Map Orientation

Each of the road maps is oriented with north pointing towards the top of the page. The 3D maps are presented from either a southeast or southwest point of view. The north arrow on each map indicates its' orientation. The 3D maps are rotated and scaled to provide the best possible view of the routes being profiled, and of some of the surrounding terrain.

# North and South Bay Area Index Maps

**T**here is a whole world full of great bike routes, and the maps in this book will help you find some of the best in the San Francisco Bay Area. The two maps on the following pages allow you to locate rides in a specific area of interest. The numbered boxes on these index maps are keyed to the numbers on the route maps throughout the book and in the table of contents. The route maps contain detailed information about rides in an area, and also show other roads that are good for cycling.

North Bay Area
Index Map
(pages 20-21)

South Bay Area
Index Map
(pages 22-23)

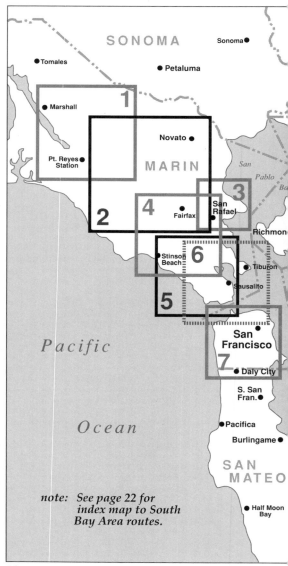

SONOMA

● Sonoma

● Tomales

● Petaluma

**1**

● Marshall

Novato ●

**2**

MARIN

Pt. Reyes ●
Station

*San*

*Pablo*

*Ba*

**3**

**4**

Fairfax ●

San
Rafael

Richmon

Stinson
Beach

**6**

● Tiburon

**5**

Sausalito ●

*Pacific*

San
Francisco

**7**

● Daly City

*Ocean*

S. San
Fran. ●

● Pacifica

Burlingame ●

SAN
MATEO

*note: See page 22 for
index map to South
Bay Area routes.*

● Half Moon
Bay

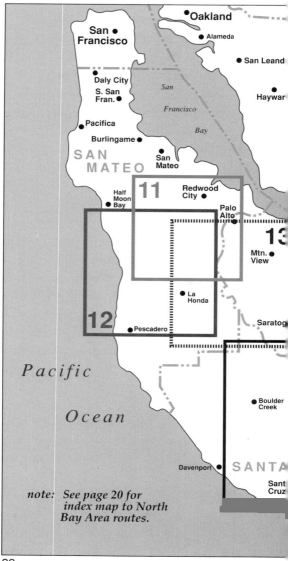

Oakland

San Francisco

Alameda

San Leand

Daly City

San

S. San Fran.

Francisco

Haywar

Pacifica

Bay

Burlingame

SAN

San

MATEO

Mateo

**11**

Redwood City

Half Moon Bay

Palo Alto

**13**

Mtn. View

**12**

La Honda

Saratog

Pescadero

*Pacific*

*Ocean*

Boulder Creek

Davenport

SANTA

Sant Cruz

*note: See page 20 for index map to North Bay Area routes.*

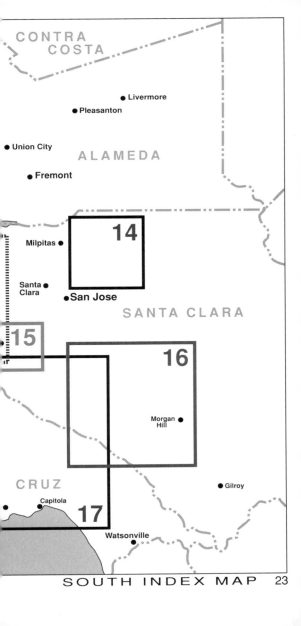

CONTRA
COSTA

● Livermore

● Pleasanton

● Union City

ALAMEDA

● Fremont

**14**

Milpitas ●

Santa ●
Clara

●San Jose

SANTA CLARA

**15**

**16**

Morgan ●
Hill

CRUZ

● Gilroy

Capitola

**17**

Watsonville ●

# ROUTE SUMMARY

# Tomales Bay

### and

# Inverness

**P**oint Reyes Station is the starting point for both of these rides, and is a good place to find picnic supplies for the trip. Tomales Bay, flanked by hills to the east and west, is especially picturesque - at bay level from Shoreline Hwy. or Sir Francis Drake Blvd., and from the hills as you climb away from Marshall. The terrain isn't as harsh here as it is in the Marin headlands area, and the roads are less busy. Sir Francis Drake Hwy. does, however, carry a lot of traffic into the Pt. Reyes National Seashore on weekends.

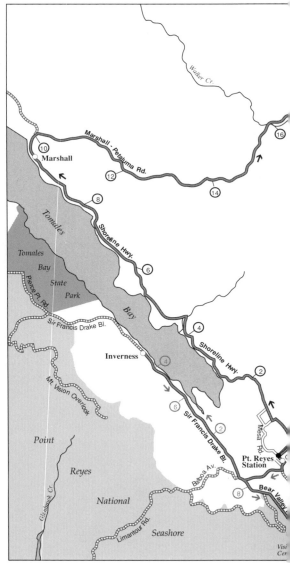

Walker Cr.

Marshall - Petaluma Rd.

(16)

(10) **Marshall**

(12)

(14)

(8)

*Tomales*

Shoreline Hwy.

*Tomales*
*Bay*

(6)

*State*

*Park*

*Bay*

Pierce Pt. Rd.

Sir Francis Drake Bl.

(4)

**Inverness**

Shoreline Hwy.

(4)

(2)

Mt. Vision Overlook

(6) Sir Francis Drake Bl.

(2)

Mesa Rd.

**Point**

**Pt. Reyes**
**Station**

Glenbrook Cr.

**Reyes**

Balboa Av.

**National**

(8)

**Bear Valley**

Limantour Rd.

*Seashore*

Visi
Cer

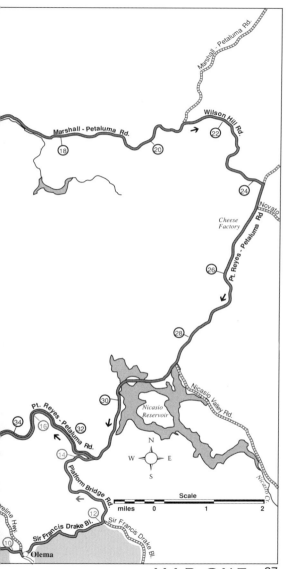

Marshall - Petaluma Rd.

Marshall - Petaluma Rd.

Wilson Hill Rd.

18

20

22

24

Cheese
Factory

Pt. Reyes - Petaluma Rd.

Novato

26

28

30

Nicasio Valley Rd.

Nicasio
Reservoir

Pt. Reyes - Petaluma Rd.

34

16

32

14

Platform Bridge Rd.

N
W    E
S

Nicasio Cr.

Scale

miles    0    1    2

reline Hwy.

Sir Francis Drake Bl.

Sir Francis Drake Bl.

12

10

Olema

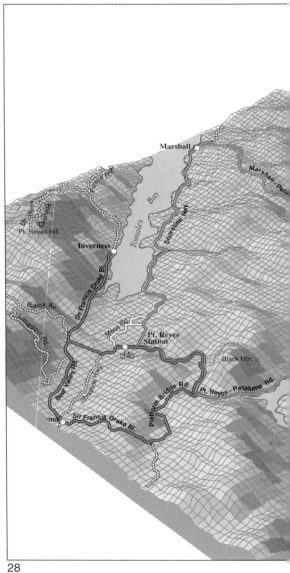

Marshall

Marshall -Peta

Tomales Bay

Shoreline Hwy.

Mt. Vision
Overlook
Pt. Reyes Hill

Inverness

Petra P. Rd.

Sir Francis Drake Bl.

Balboa Av.

Limantour Rd.

Mesa Rd.

Pt. Reyes
Station

Black Mtn.

Bear Valley Rd.

Shoreline Hwy.

Platform Bridge Rd.

Pt. Reyes - Petaluma Rd.

ma

Sir Francis Drake Bl.

San
Reyes

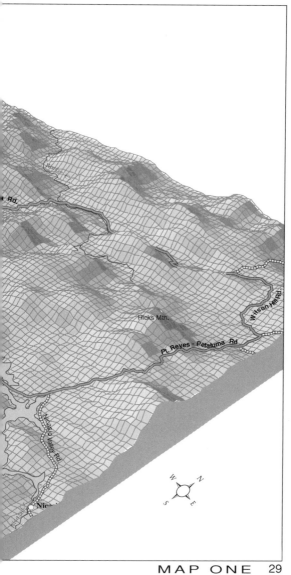

Rd.

Hicks Mtn.

Wilson Hill Rd.

Pt. Reyes - Petaluma Rd.

Nicasio Valley Rd.

Nica

# TOMALES BAY

## 35.1 miles

0    Start at Pt. Reyes Station; head north on Shoreline Hwy. (Hwy. 1)
9.0  Marshall (food).
**10.0 Turn right on Marshall - Petaluma Rd.**
**21.3 Turn right on Hicks Valley Rd. (also called Wilson Hill Rd.)**
**24.1 Turn right on Pt. Reyes - Petaluma Rd.**
24.6 Intersection with Novato Blvd.
25.0 Cheese factory.
28.5 Intersection with Nicasio Valley Rd.
31.6 Intersection with Platform Bridge Rd.
**34.6 Turn left on Shoreline Hwy. (Hwy. 1).**
35.1 End at Pt. Reyes Station.

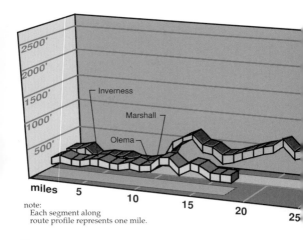

note:
Each segment along
route profile represents one mile.

30

# INVERNESS

## 17.9 miles

| | |
|---|---|
| 0 | Start at Pt. Reyes Station; head south on Shoreline Hwy. (Hwy. 1). |
| **0.4** | **Turn right on Sir Francis Drake Blvd.** |
| **4.5** | **Inverness; turn around point.** |
| 7.8 | Continue straight onto Bear Valley Rd. |
| **10.1** | **Turn right on Shoreline Hwy. (Hwy. 1).** |
| **10.2** | **Turn left on Sir Francis Drake Blvd.** |
| **12.0** | **Turn left on Platform Bridge Rd.** |
| **14.3** | **Turn left on Pt. Reyes - Petaluma Rd.** |
| **17.4** | **Turn left on Shoreline Hwy. (Hwy. 1).** |
| 17.9 | End at Pt. Reyes Station. |

### Places of Interest

**Point Reyes National Seashore.** Extensive system of trails and opportunities for off-road cycling. Beaches, wilderness area, and a wide variety of marsh to mountain habitat for wildlife and bird watching. Good vantage points for whale watching.

**National Park Visitor Center.** Exhibits and information about the Point Reyes National Seashore.

**Cheese Factory.** Sales and tours. Picnic supplies and a pleasant area to relax and enjoy it.

## Route Profiles

Portion of route in:
Urban
Suburban
Rural

Cheese factory

2500'
2000'
1500'
1000'
500'

30    35    40    45

## Routes suggested by: Kirsten Goettler

Kirsten has spent years riding the the roads of Marin County - and beyond. She is an avid cyclist who has recently participated in amateur racing in Italy, and who regularly takes on challenges such as the Davis Double and the Markleyville Death Ride.

## Notes: _____

_____

_____

_____

_____

_____


# Calorie Counter

## Route: Tomales Bay

| Average Speed (mph) | Riding Time | Calories Expended* |
|---|---|---|
| 5 | 7 hrs. 01 mins. | 1000 |
| 10 | 3 hrs. 31 mins. | 1110 |
| 15 | 2 hrs. 20 mins. | 1410 |
| 20 | 1 hr. 45 mins. | 1930 |

## Route: Inverness

| Average Speed (mph) | Riding Time | Calories Expended* |
|---|---|---|
| 5 | 3 hrs. 35 mins. | 480 |
| 10 | 1 hr. 47 mins. | 510 |
| 15 | 1 hr. 12 mins. | 630 |
| 20 | 54 mins. | 910 |

* Estimations from tractive-resistance calculations
Whitt and Wilson, "Bicycling Science"

# Nicasio

### and

# Lucas Valley

**T**hese rides explore some of the rolling hill country closest to the populated area of East Marin. There are some nice contrasts in the environment along these two routes, ranging from heavily forested to open grassland. Sir Francis Drake Blvd. carries quite a bit of traffic to the Pt. Reyes area, especially on weekends, and some extra caution should be exercised. Lucas Valley Road twists and turns through a sometimes narrow canyon before emerging into the suburbs of Terra Linda. From there, a paved trail across the ridge provides the link to the street system leading into Fairfax.

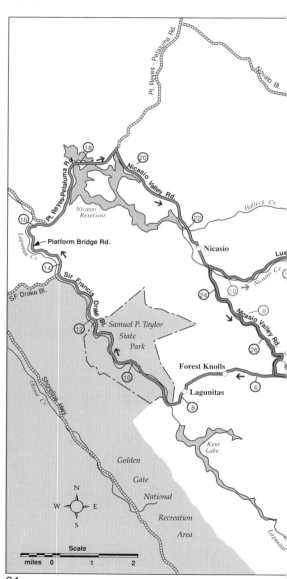

Pt. Reyes - Petaluma Rd.

Novato Bl.

⑱

⑳ Nicasio Valley Rd.

Halleck Cr.

Pt. Reyes-Petaluma Rd.

Nicasio Reservoir

⑯

Lagunitas Cr.

Platform Bridge Rd.

⑭

SF Drake Bl.

Sir Francis Drake Bl.

⑫

Samuel P. Taylor State Park

⑩

⑧

Shoreline Hwy.

Olema Cr.

Golden

Gate

National

Recreation

Area

N W E S

Scale

miles 0 1 2

㉒

Nicasio

Luc

Nicasio Cr.

㉔ ⑩

⑧

Nicasio Valley Rd.

㉖

Forest Knolls

⑥

⑧ Lagunitas

Kent Lake

Lagunitas

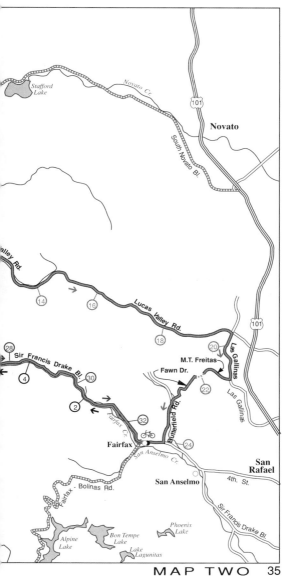

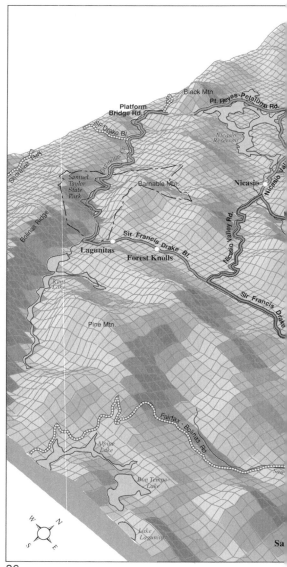

Black Mtn

Platform
Bridge Rd.

Pt. Reyes-Petaluma Rd.

SF Drake Bl.

Shoreline Hwy

Nicasio
Reservoir

Samuel
Taylor
State
Park

Lagunitas Creek

Barnable Mtn

Nicasio

Nicasio Valley

Bolinas Ridge

Lagunitas

Sir Francis Drake Bl.

Forest Knolls

Nicasio Valley Rd.

Kent
Lake

Sir Francis Drake

Pine Mtn.

Fairfax - Bolinas Rd.

Alpine
Lake

San

Don Tempo
Lake

Lake
Lagunitas

Sa

N
W        E
S

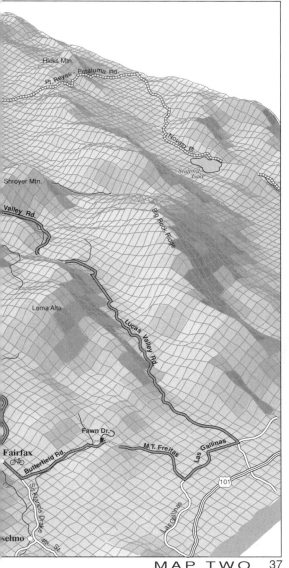

Hicks Mtn.

Pt Reyes - Petaluma  Rd.

Nokarp R.

Stafford Lake

Shroyer Mtn.

Valley   Rd.

Big Rock Ridge

Loma Alta

Lucas   Valley   Rd.

Fawn Dr.

Fairfax

Butterfield Rd.

M.T. Freitas

Las Gallinas

101

Sir Francis Drake  Blv.   St.

Las Gallinas

selmo

# NICASIO

## 32.6 miles

0   Start at Fairfax town center parking lot; head NW
    on Sir Francis Drake Blvd.
5.4  Intersection with Nicasio Valley Rd.
6.9  Forest Knolls (food).
7.8  Laqunitas (food).
8.5  Enter Samuel P. Taylor State Park.
9.8  Leave road to join alternate bike path.
10.3 Entrance to campground, visitor center, picnic
    areas, etc. (phone, restrooms, water).
12.1 Leave park.
**13.8 Turn right on Platform Bridge Rd.** (not marked -
    turns just before road crosses bridge and goes
    uphill).
16.2 Continue straight onto Pt. Reyes-Petaluma Rd.
**19.3 Turn right on Nicosio Valley Rd.**
23.3 Intersection with Lucas Valley Rd.
**27.2 Turn left on Sir Francis Drake Blvd.**
32.6 End at Fairfax town center parking lot.

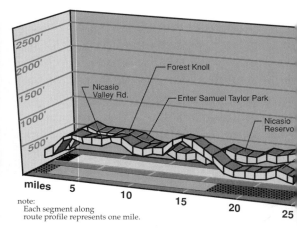

note:
Each segment along
route profile represents one mile.

# LUCAS VALLEY

## 24.6 miles

0    Leave Fairfax town center parking lot; head NW
      on Sir Francis Drake Blvd.
**5.4   Turn right on Nicasio Valley Rd.**
**9.3   Turn right on Lucas Valley Rd.**
**19.3 Turn right on Las Gallinas Ave.**
**20.6 Turn right on Manuel Freitas Blvd.**
21.9 Continue onto Mission Path Trail.
**22.2 Turn right at end of trail onto Fawn Dr.**
**22.8 Turn left on Butterfield Rd.**
**24.0 Turn right on Sir Francis Drake Blvd.**
24.6 End at Fairfax town center parking lot.

---

### Places of Interest

**Samuel P. Taylor State Park**. Well known recreation
area since the 1870's. 3 mile paved bicycle trail along
former railroad right-of-way. Special camping area
for bicyclists. Off-road cycling on dirt roads
throughout the park. Swimming and picnicking.
Visitor center. Wide variety in the natural landscape,
from lush canyon bottoms to open grasslands.
Annual migration of silver salmon and steelhead up
Lagunitas (Papermill) Creek.

---

# Route Profiles

**Portion of route in:**
Urban
Suburban
Rural

Mission Path Trail

2500'
2000'
1500'
1000'
500'

30     35     40     45

### Routes suggested by:
### Mick Coyle

After years of living and working in Marin County, Mick has an extensive inventory of bike rides to draw on. As owner of Mike's Bicycle Center, 1601 Fourth Street, San Rafael, he is in constant contact with area cyclists and keeps up with Marin's cycling scene.

**Notes:** _____

_____

_____

_____

_____

_____

# Calorie Counter

### Route: Nicasio

| Average Speed (mph) | Riding Time | Calories Expended* |
| --- | --- | --- |
| 5 | 6 hrs. 31 mins. | 890 |
| 10 | 3 hrs. 15 mins. | 990 |
| 15 | 2 hrs. 10 mins. | 1250 |
| 20 | 1 hr. 38 mins. | 1720 |

### Route: Lucas Valley

| Average Speed (mph) | Riding Time | Calories Expended* |
| --- | --- | --- |
| 5 | 4 hrs. 55 mins. | 690 |
| 10 | 2 hrs. 28 mins. | 760 |
| 15 | 1 hr. 38 mins. | 910 |
| 20 | 1 hr. 14 mins. | 1320 |

\* Estimations from tractive-resistance calculations
Whitt and Wilson, "Bicycling Science"

# San Pedro Point
## and
# Around China Camp

The road through China Camp State Park offers a refreshing respite from the otherwise intensely developed East Marin. The sweeping architecture of the Marin Civic Center puts you in the right frame of mind for the peaceful ride along San Pablo Bay. Once you have passed McNear's Beach, you are back in a suburban setting. The climb up Margarita Dr. and Highland Ave. is short and steep, and lends a little variation to an otherwise fairly flat ride. Bay Hills Dr. on the north side of the peninsula offers a challenging climb into the hills of the park.

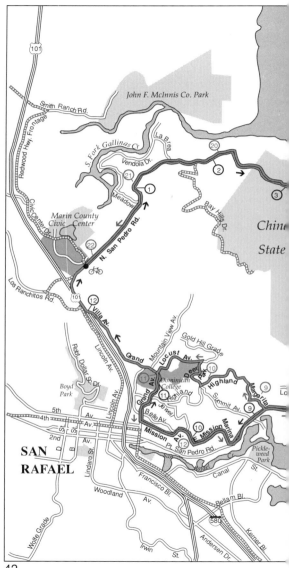

John F. McInnis Co. Park

Smith Ranch Rd.

Redwood Hwy. Frontage

S. Fork Gallinas Cr.

La Brea

Vendola Dr.

20

21

2

Meadow

3

Civic Center Dr.

Marin County
Civic Center

Bay Hills Dr.

Chine

1

State

22

N. San Pedro Rd.

Los Ranchitos Rd.

101

12

Villa Av.

Mountain View Av.

Gold Hill Grade

Grand

Robt. Dollar Dr.

Lincoln Av.

Locust Av.

Deer Pk.

10

Boyd
Park

Dominican
College

Highland

Highland Av.

Margarita

9

4th Av.

Grand Av.

Jewel

Summit Av.

9

Lo

2nd Av.

Belle Av.

Marina

10

B St.

A St.

Mission Av.

E. Mission

Pickle-
weed
Park

SAN
RAFAEL

Lindaro St.

12

Pt. San Pedro Rd.

Canal
St.

Woodland Av.

Francisco Bl.

Rafael Canal

Bellam Bl.

Wolfe Grade

580

Kerner Bl.

Irwin St.

Andersen Dr.

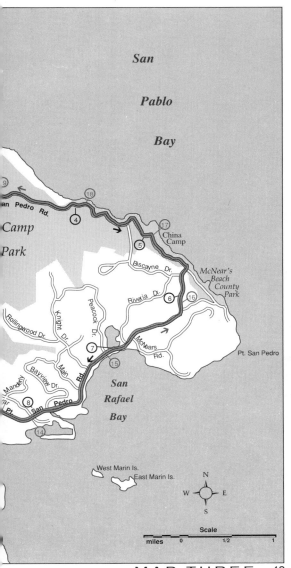

San

Pablo

Bay

⑨
an Pedro Rd. ⑱
④
⑰
Camp China
Camp
Park ⑤
Biscayne Dr.
McNear's
Beach
Riveria Dr. County
⑥ Park
Knight Dr. ⑯
Rollingwood Dr. Peacock Dr.
McNears
⑦ Rd.
Pt. San Pedro
Bayview Dr. ⑮
Main Rd.
Mandvi
⑧ San Pedro San
al Pt. San Pedro Rafael
⑭ Bay

West Marin Is.
East Marin Is.
N
W ⊕ E
S

Scale
miles 0 1/2 1

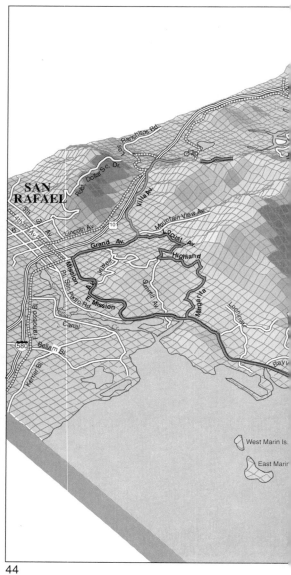

SAN RAFAEL

Robt. Dollar Sc. Dr.

Los Ranchitos Rd.

Villa Av.

5th Av.
4th Av.
Lincoln Av.
101
Grand Av.
Mountain View Av.
Locust Av.
Highland
Mission
Ida Well Av.
E. Mission
Mission
Pt. San Pedro Rd.
Sanmil Av.
Margarita
Lochinvar
Canal
Bay V.
Francisco Bl.
580
Bellam Bl.
Kerner Bl.

West Marin Is.

East Marin

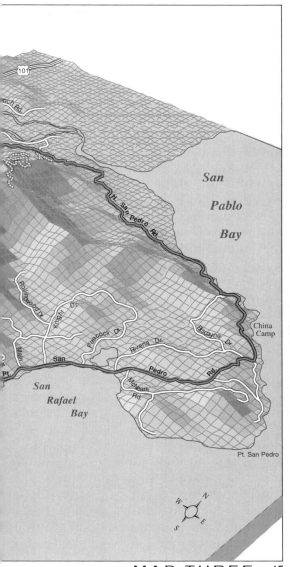

101

nch Rd.

N. San Pedro Rd.

*San*

*Pablo*

*Bay*

Rollingwood Dr.

Knight Dr.

Peacock Dr.

Riviera Dr.

Biscayne Dr.

China
Camp

Main

San

Pt.

Pedro Rd.

McNears Rd.

*San*

*Rafael*

*Bay*

Pt. San Pedro

N
W — E
S

# SAN PEDRO POINT
## 22.1 miles

| | |
|---|---|
| 0 | Start at Marin County Civic Center; **turn left and head NE on North San Pedro Rd.;** becomes Pt. San Pedro Rd. |
| 2.7 | Enter China Camp State Park. |
| 5.2 | China Camp Village. |
| 6.2 | Entrance to McNear's Beach County Park. |
| **8.9** | **Turn right on Margarita Dr.** |
| **9.4** | **Turn left on Highland Ave.** |
| **10.1** | **Turn right on Deer Park Ave.** |
| **10.4** | **Turn left on Locust Ave.** |
| **11.0** | **Turn left on Grand Ave.** |
| **11.5** | **Turn left on Mission Ave.** |
| **12.2** | **Turn left on E. Mission Ave.** |
| **12.7** | **Turn left on Pt. San Pedro Rd.** |
| 13.2 | Intersection with Margarita Dr. |
| 22.1 | End at Marin County Civic Center. |

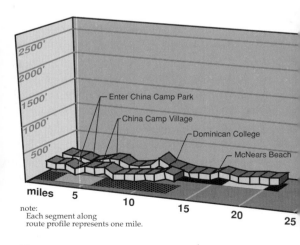

note:
Each segment along
route profile represents one mile.

# AROUND CHINA CAMP

## 12.8 miles

0   Start at Marin County Civic Center; **turn left and head NE on North San Pedro Rd.;** becomes Pt. San Pedro Rd.
2.7  Enter China Camp State Park.
5.2  China Camp Village.
6.2  Entrance to McNear's Beach County Park.
8.9  Intersection with Margarita Dr.
**9.4  Turn right on E. Mission Ave. (Marina).**
**9.9  Turn right on Mission Ave.**
**10.6 Turn right on Grand Ave.**
11.1 Intersection with Locust Ave.
12.0 Join Hwy. 101.
12.4 Exit Hwy. 101.
12.8 End at Marin County Civic Center.

---

### Places of Interest

**China Camp State Park.** 1,500 acres of rolling hills, meadows and marshlands. Hiking, walking, swimming, wading and picnicking.

**China Camp.** Historic shrimp fishing village. Visitor center open on weekends.

**McNear's Beach County Park.** Swimming, sunbathing, picnicking.

**Marin County Civic Center.** Imaginative architecture of Frank Lloyd Wright.

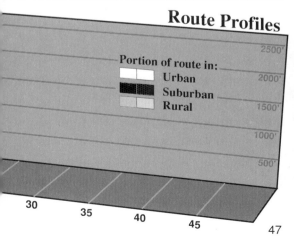

## Route Profiles

Portion of route in:
Urban
Suburban
Rural

2500'
2000'
1500'
1000'
500'

30    35    40    45

## Routes suggested by: Kirsten Goettler

Kirsten has spent years riding the the roads of Marin County - and beyond. She is an avid cyclist who has recently participated in amateur racing in Italy, and who regularly takes on challenges such as the Davis Double and the Markleyville Death Ride.

## Notes: _____

_____

_____

_____

_____

_____

# Calorie Counter

### Route: San Pedro Point

| Average Speed (mph) | Riding Time | Calories Expended* |
|---|---|---|
| 5 | 4 hrs. 25 mins. | 610 |
| 10 | 2 hrs. 13 mins. | 660 |
| 15 | 1 hr. 28 mins. | 780 |
| 20 | 1 hr. 6 mins. | 1150 |

### Route: Around China Camp

| Average Speed (mph) | Riding Time | Calories Expended* |
|---|---|---|
| 5 | 2 hrs. 34 mins. | 350 |
| 10 | 1 hr. 17 mins. | 380 |
| 15 | 51 mins. | 460 |
| 20 | 38 mins. | 670 |

* Estimations from tractive-resistance calculations
Whitt and Wilson, "Bicycling Science"

# Mt. Tamalpais

### and

# Alpine Lake

**U**nless you are on a mountain bike, there isn't a good alternative to the out-and-back Alpine Lake route for a short loop ride from Fairfax into Mt. Tamalpais State Park. And making it to the summit of the East Peak is a challenging ride from any direction. The rolling and open landscape along W. Ridgecrest Blvd. is the setting for one of the most picturesque portions of any ride in this book, with breathtaking views overlooking Bolinas Lagoon and the Pacific Ocean. Mt. Tamalpais well known as the home of mountain biking, and many trails in the park are open for off-road riding.

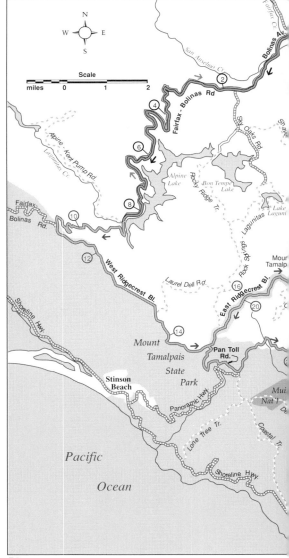

N
W E
S

Scale
miles  0   1   2

Fafida Cr.

Bolinas Av.

San Anselmo Cr.

④

②

Fairfax - Bolinas Rd

Sky Oaks Rd.

Shaver

⑥

Alpine - Kent Pump Rd.

Lagunitas Cr.

Alpine Lake

Rocky Ridge Tr.

Bon Tempe Lake

Lake Laguni

⑧

⑩

Fairfax - Bolinas Rd.

⑫

West Ridgecrest Bl.

Rock Spring Rd.

Laurel Dell Rd.

Lagunitas

⑯

Mour Tamalp

East Ridgecrest Bl.

⑳

⑭

Mount Tamalpais State Park

Pan Toll Rd.

Shoreline Hwy.

Stinson Beach

Panoramic Hwy.

Mui Nat'l

Lone Tree Tr.

Coastal Tr.

De

Pacific Ocean

Shoreline Hwy.

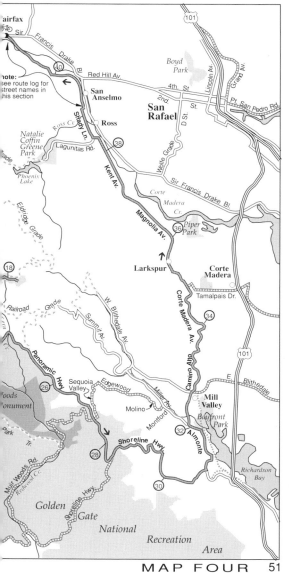

Fairfax

note:
see route log for
street names in
this section

Sir Francis Drake Bl.

Red Hill Av.

San Anselmo

Ross

Natalie
Coffin
Greene
Park

Ross Cr.

Shady Ln.

Lagunitas Rd.

Phoenix
Lake

Eldridge Grade

Kent Av.

Magnolia Av.

Larkspur

Boyd
Park

4th. St.

2nd.
St.

San
Rafael

D St.

Lincoln Av.

Grand Av.

Pt. San Pedro Rd.

Wolfe Grade

Sir Francis Drake Bl.

Corte
Madera
Cr.

Piper
Park

Corte
Madera

Tamalpais Dr.

Corte Madera Av.

Camino Alto

101

Railroad

Grade

Summit Av.

W. Blithedale Av.

Panoramic Hwy.

Sequoia
Valley

Edgewood

Molino

Miller Av.

Montford

Almonte

Mill
Valley

Bayfront
Park

E. Blithedale

Richardson
Bay

oods
onument

Muir Woods Rd.

Redwood Cr.

Shoreline Hwy.

Shoreline Hwy.

Golden

Gate

National

Recreation

Area

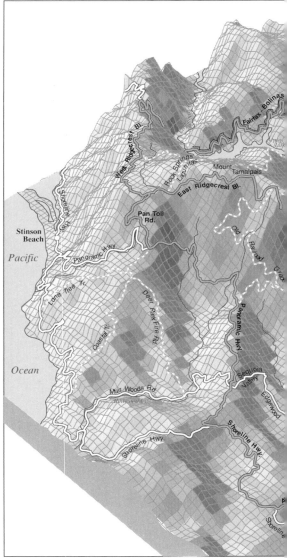

Pacific

Ocean

Stinson
Beach

West Ridgecrest Bl.

Rock Springs
Lagunitas

Mount
Tamalpais

East Ridgecrest Bl.

Fairfax Bolinas

Alpine
Lake

Pan Toll
Rd.

Shoreline Hwy.

Panoramic Hwy.

Lone Tree Tr.

Coastal Tr.

Deer Park Fire Rd.

Muir Woods Rd.

Redwood Cr.

Old Railroad Grade

Lagunitas Creek

Panoramic Hwy.

Sequoia
Valley

Edgewood

Shoreline Hwy.

Shoreline Hwy.

Shoreline

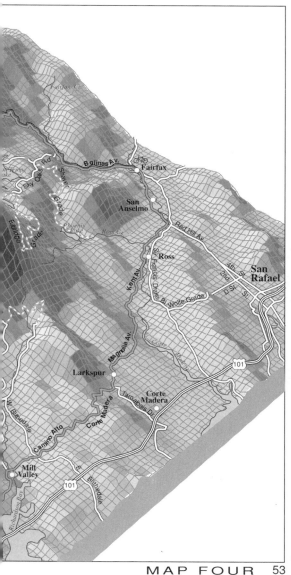

# MT. TAMALPAIS

## 41.3 miles

0     Start at Broadway Ave. and Bolinas Rd. in Fairfax;
      head SW on Bolinas Av.; becomes Bolinas-
      Fairfax Rd.
8.5   Dam at Alpine Lake.
**11.1  Bear left onto W. Ridgecrest Blvd.** (not marked - do
      not start descending).
**15.2  Bear left onto E. Ridgecrest Blvd. to Mt. Tamalpais.**
18.3  Mt. Tamalpais parking lot (toilets, water, phone,
      trails to top of peak); **turn around point.**
**21.4  Bear left onto Pan Toll Rd.**
**22.9  Bear left onto Panoramic Hwy.**
27.5  Intersection with Muir Woods Rd.
**28.5  Bear left onto Shoreline Hwy. (Hwy. 1).**
**31.2  Turn left on Almonte Blvd.**
**32.1  Turn right on Camino Alto;** becomes Corte-
      Madera Ave.
35.1  Continue straight onto Magnolia Ave.
**37.4  Bear left onto Kent Ave.; becomes Poplar Ave.**
**38.4  Turn left on Lagunitas Rd.**
      **Turn right on Shady Lane.**
      **Turn right on Bolinas Ave.**
      **Turn left on San Anselmo;** pick up Bike Route
      signs.
      **Turn left on street parallel to Center Blvd.**
      Join Center Blvd. at Pastori Ave.
41.3  End at Broadway Ave. and Bolinas Rd.

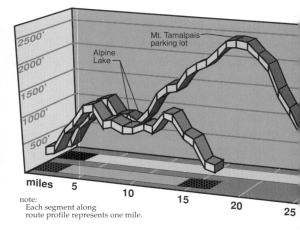

note:
Each segment along
route profile represents one mile.

54

# ALPINE LAKE

## 17 miles

0   Start at Broadway Ave. and Bolinas Rd. in Fairfax; head SW on Bolinas Rd.; becomes Bolinas-Fairfax Rd.

**8.5  Dam at Alpine Lake; turn around point.**
*    Note: Return over the same route.*

17.0 End at Broadway Ave. and Bolinas Rd.

---

### Places of Interest

**Mt. Tamalpais Summit.** 360 degree panorama of the region.

**Muir Woods National Monument.** Virgin coast redwood stand, visitor center, nature trail, and hiking trails.

**Golden Gate National Recreation Area.** Many miles of hiking and off-road cycling trails in undeveloped parkland.

**Mt. Tamalpais State Park.** Hiking and off-road cycling trails, camping.

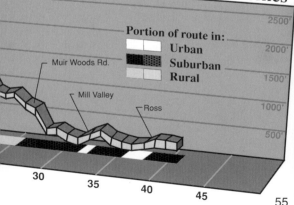

## Route Profiles

### Routes suggested by:
### Liz Coyle

Liz has ridden the hills of Marin County for years, and has drawn on that experience when touring in Europe, the Rockies and the Northwest. While she enjoys the chall- enge of a steep hill climb or a Markleyville Death Ride, she is certainly not adverse to an easier ride.

## Notes:

# Calorie Counter

### Route:  Mt. Tamalpais

| Average Speed (mph) | Riding Time | Calories Expended* |
|---|---|---|
| 5 | 8 hrs. 16 mins. | 1130 |
| 10 | 4 hrs.  8 mins. | 1250 |
| 15 | 2 hrs. 45 mins. | 1580 |
| 20 | 2 hrs.  4 mins. | 2170 |

### Route:  Alpine Lake

| Average Speed (mph) | Riding Time | Calories Expended* |
|---|---|---|
| 5 | 3 hrs. 24 mins. | 470 |
| 10 | 1 hr.  42 mins. | 520 |
| 15 | 1 hr.  8 mins. | 620 |
| 20 | 51 mins. | 900 |

\* Estimations from tractive-resistance calculations
Whitt and Wilson, "Bicycling Science"

# Panoramic Hwy.

### and

# Muir Woods

These two rides take you from the Golden Gate Bridge into the heart of West Marin. The undeveloped lands of the Golden Gate National Recreation Area lie in stark contrast to the intensity of the eastern half of the county. It's a truly beautiful area, for both on- and off-road cycling. There is a lot of traffic on these roads, especially on weekends, because of the popularity and proximity of the Pacific beaches, Muir Woods National Monument, and Mount Tamalpais. The Sequoia Valley/ Edgewood Rd. alternate route is a good way to avoid the traffic on a section of Shoreline Hwy.

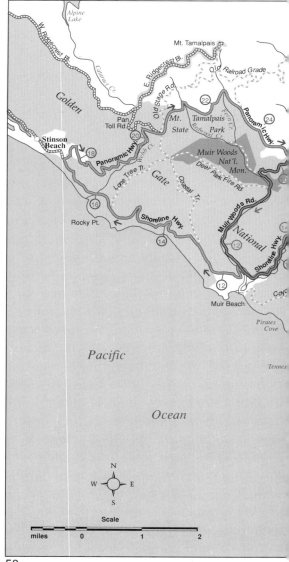

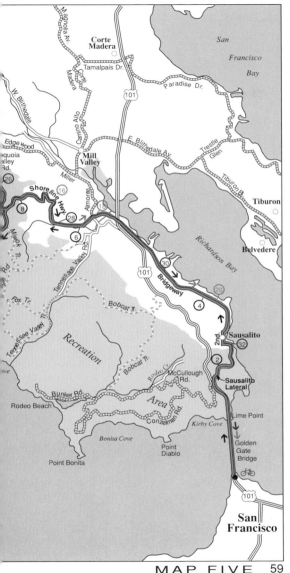

San
Francisco
Bay

Corte
Madera

Magnolia Av.

Madera

Tamalpais Dr.

Paradise Dr.

101

W. Blithedale

Camino Alto

E. Blithedale Av.

Trestle
Glen

Tiburon Bl.

Edge wood

equoia
alley
Rd.

26

Mill
Valley

Miller

Almonte

Tiburon

Shoreline Hwy

8

28

16

19

6

Belvedere

Miwok Tr.

Tennessee Valley Rd.

Fox Tr.

Bobcat Tr.

Richardson Bay

30

101

Bridgeway

20

4

Tennessee Valley Tr.

Recreation

Bobcat Tr.

2nd.

Sausalito

32

2

ove

Bunker Rd.

Rodeo Cr.

McCullough
Rd.

Sausalito
Lateral

Area

Conzelman Rd.

Rodeo Beach

Bonita Cove

Lime Point

Kirby Cove

Point
Diablo

Golden
Gate
Bridge

Point Bonita

101

San
Francisco

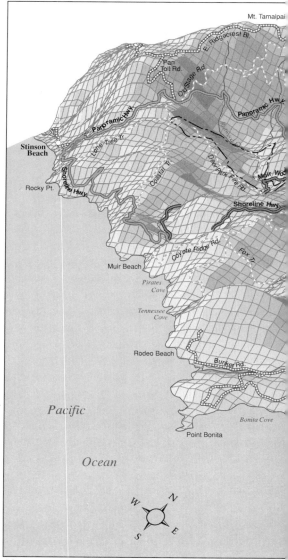

Mt. Tamalpai

E. Ridgecrest Bl.

Pan
Toll Rd.

Old Stage Rd.

Panoramic Hwy

Panoramic Hwy

Lone Tree Tr.

Stinson
Beach

Coastal Tr.

Deer Park Fire Rd.

Muir Wo

Shoreline Hwy

Rocky Pt.

Shoreline Hwy

Shoreline Hwy

Coyote Ridge Rd.

Fox Tr.

Muir Beach

Pirates
Cove

Tennessee
Cove

Rodeo Beach

Bunker Rd.

Pacific

Bonita Cove

Point Bonita

Ocean

W    N    E    S

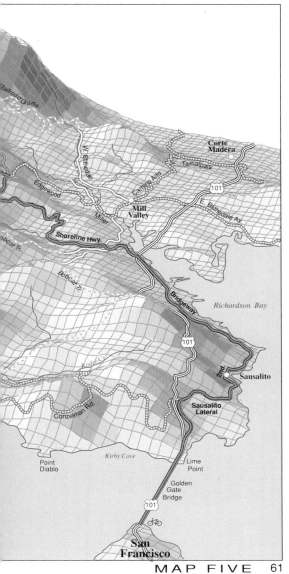

Railroad Grade

Corte
Madera

W. Blithedale

Edgewood

Tamalpais

Camino Alto

101

Miller

E. Blithedale Av

Mill
Valley

Shoreline Hwy.

Bobcat Tr.

Bobcat Tr.

Bridgeway

Richardson Bay

101

Rodeo CV

2nd

Sausalito

Conzelman Rd.

Sausalito
Lateral

101

Kirby Cove

Lime
Point

Point
Diablo

Golden
Gate
Bridge

101

San
Francisco

# PANORAMIC HWY.
## 34.9 miles

0     Start at the south end of the Golden Gate Bridge.
1.7   Enter Vista Point; leave the parking lot on the bicycle path.
1.9   Join Sausalito Lateral., becomes Alexander Ave., then 2nd St., then Bridgeway as it works its way through Sausalito.
5.4   Join bike path paralleling Bridgeway; path separates from road at Gate 6 Rd. and loops around under Hwy. 101.; **bear left at fork in path just before footbridge.**
5.7   Join Shoreline Hwy. (Hwy. 1) near Almonte Blvd.
8.4   Intersection with Panoramic Hwy.
10.9  Intersection with Pacific Hwy.; 1/4 mile to beach (phone, toilets).
11.2  Intersection with Muir Woods Rd.
**17.1  Turn right on Panoramic Hwy.;** 1/2 mile straight to Stinson Beach (food, toilets, phone).
20.8  Intersection with Pan Toll Rd.; Park Headquarters on right (phone, toilets, campground).
25.5  Intersection with Muir Woods Rd.
**26.5  Bear left onto Shoreline Hwy. (Hwy. 1)**
**29.2  Turn left on bikepath near Almonte Blvd. and follow until joining Bridgeway;** continue on Bridgeway through Sausalito to Hwy. 101; cross the Golden Gate Bridge on the side designated for cyclists.
34.9  End at the south end of the Golden Gate Bridge.

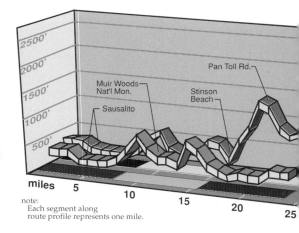

note:
Each segment along route profile represents one mile.

# MUIR WOODS

## 23.7 miles

0-5.7 Same directions as for Panoramic Hwy. loop.
**8.4 Turn right on Panoramic Hwy.**
**9.4 Turn left on Muir Woods Rd.**
10.9 Entrance to Muir Woods National Monument
(food, phone, toilets, water).
**12.5 Turn left on Shoreline Hwy. (Hwy. 1)**
12.8 Intersection with Pacific Hwy.; 1/4 mile to beach
(phone, toilets).
15.3 Intersection with Panoramic Hwy.
**18.0 Turn left on bikepath near Almonte Blvd. and**
**follow until joining Bridgeway;** continue on
Bridgeway through Sausalito to Hwy. 101; cross
the Golden Gate Bridge on the side designated
for cyclists.
23.7 End at the south end of the Golden Gate Bridge.

---

### Places of Interest

**Muir Woods National Monument.** Virgin coast
redwood and Douglas fir stands. Hiking, visitor center.

**Golden Gate National Recreation Area and Mt.
Tamalpais State Park.** Extensive system of trails for
hiking and off-road cycling. Variety of terrain and
vegetation covering the Marin headlands.

**Muir Beach.** Picnicking, beachcombing, wading,
sunbathing. Unsafe for swimming.

**Stinson Beach.** Swimming, wading, sunbathing.

---

# Route Profiles

Portion of route in:
Urban
Suburban
Rural

Muir Woods Rd.

Sausalito

2500'
2000'
1500'
1000'
500'

30   35   40   45

**Routes suggested by:**
**David Goettler**

As the owner of four bicycle stores in the Bay Area, and a resident of Marin County, David is familiar with bike routes throughout the region. His Pacific Bicycle stores are located at 1161 Sutter in San Francisco, 2701 College in Berkeley, 2409 J St. in Sacramento, and 1040 Grant, #105 in Mountain View.

**Notes:** _____

_____

_____

_____

_____

_____

# Calorie Counter

### Route: Panoramic Hwy.

| Average Speed (mph) | Riding Time | Calories Expended* |
|---|---|---|
| 5 | 6 hrs. 59 mins. | 1000 |
| 10 | 3 hrs. 29 mins. | 1110 |
| 15 | 2 hrs. 20 mins. | 1410 |
| 20 | 1 hr. 45 mins. | 1930 |

### Route: Muir Woods

| Average Speed (mph) | Riding Time | Calories Expended* |
|---|---|---|
| 5 | 4 hrs. 44 mins. | 800 |
| 10 | 2 hrs. 22 mins. | 870 |
| 15 | 1 hr. 35 mins. | 1040 |
| 20 | 1 hr. 11 mins. | 1520 |

* Estimations from tractive-resistance calculations
Whitt and Wilson, "Bicycling Science"

# Tiburon

### and

# Angel Island

L ower Marin County has two distinct faces, and two completely different kinds of cycling opportunities to offer. These routes explore the residential and commercial side of the county. In contrast to the parklands of West Marin, you will find fewer and smaller hills and many places to get off your bike for food and refreshment. Sausalito and Tiburon are attractive bayside towns that overlook a scenic shoreline and constant boating activity. Contact the Red and White Ferries at (415) 546-2815 for schedules to Angel Is.

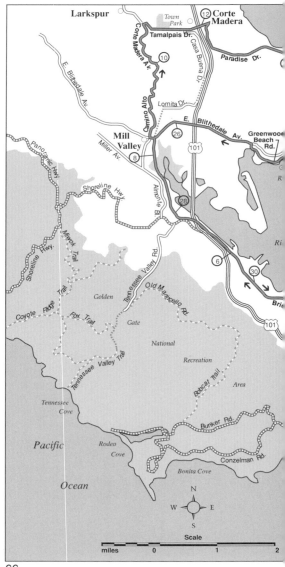

Larkspur

Town Park

12 Corte Madera

Tamalpais Dr.

Corte Madera Av.

E. Blithedale Av.

Casa Buena Dr.

Paradise Dr.

10

Lomita Dr.

Camino Alto

E. Blithedale Av.

Greenwood Beach Rd.

Mill Valley

26

101

Miller Av.

8

Panoramic Hwy.

Shoreline Hwy.

Almonte Bl.

28

R

Ri

Miwok Trail

6

Shoreline Hwy.

30

Coyote Ridge Trail

Golden

Tennessee Valley Rd.

Old Marincello Rd.

Bri

Fox Trail

Gate

101

National

Valley Trail

Tennessee Trail

Recreation

Area

Bobcat Trail

Tennessee Cove

Pacific

Rodeo Cove

Bunker Rd.

Conzelman Rd.

Bonita Cove

Ocean

N

W — E

S

Scale

miles   0                    1                    2

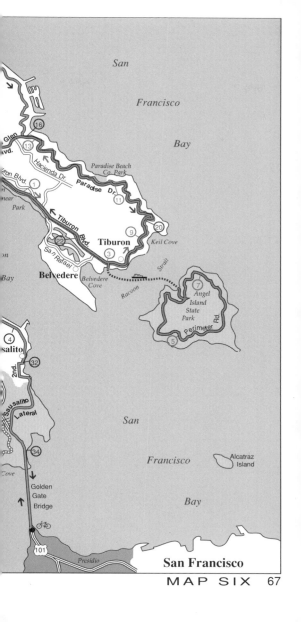

San

Francisco

Bay

Glen

vd.

Hacienda Dr.

Paradise Beach Co. Park

Paradise Dr.

Tiburon Blvd.

near Park

Tiburon Blvd.

**Tiburon**

Keil Cove

San Rafael

**Belvedere**

Belvedere Cove

Racoon

Strait

Angel Island State Park

Perimeter Rd.

alito

2nd.

Sausalito Lateral

Cove

Golden Gate Bridge

San

Francisco

Alcatraz Island

Bay

Presidio

**San Francisco**

MAP SIX 67

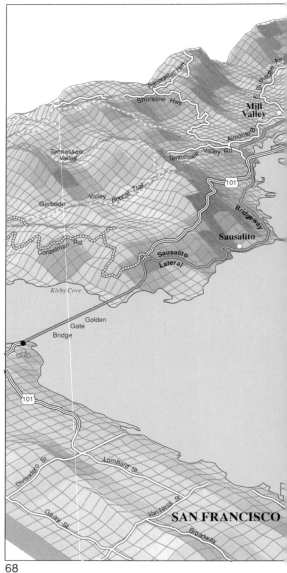

Panoramic Hwy

Shoreline Hwy

**Mill Valley**

El Blithedale Av.

Almonte

Tennessee Valley Rd.

Tennessee Valley

101

Valley

Bobcat Trail

Gerbode

Bridgeway

Conzelman Rd.

**Sausalito**

Sausalito Lateral

Kirby Cove

Golden
Gate
Bridge

101

Divisadero St.

Lombard St.

Geary St.

Van Ness St.

**SAN FRANCISCO**

Broadway

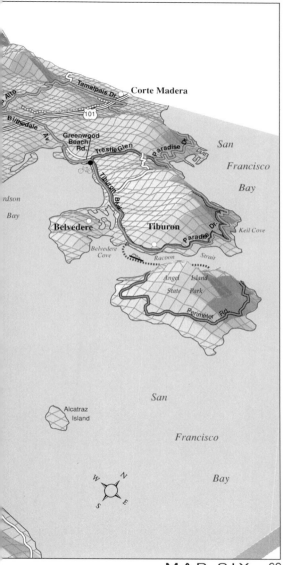

Corte Madera

**Corte Madera**

Tamalpais Dr.

Alto

Blithedale

101

Greenwood
Beach
Rd.

Trestle Glen

Paradise

Av.

San

Francisco

Bay

rdson

Bay

**Belvedere**

Belvedere
Cove

**Tiburon**

Tiburon Blvd.

Paradise Dr.

Keil Cove

Racoon    Strait

Angel    Island

State    Park

Perimeter Rd.

San

Alcatraz
Island

Francisco

Bay

W    N    E

S

# TIBURON
## 35.4 miles

0   Start at the south end of the Golden Gate Bridge; head north across the bridge.
1.7  Enter Vista Point; leave the parking lot on the bicycle path.
1.9  Join Sausalito Lateral, becomes Alexander Ave., then 2nd St., then Bridgeway.
5.4  Join bike path paralleling Bridgeway; path separates from road at Gate 6 Rd. and loops around under Hwy. 101. Follow the main bike path through park to E. Blithedale Ave.
**8.6  Cross E. Blithedale Ave. and turn left.**
**8.7  Turn right on Camino Alto;** becomes Corte Madera.
**11.2  Turn right on Redwood;** becomes Tamalpais Dr.
**12.3  Turn right on Paradise Dr. after crossing Hwy. 101.**
15.9  Intersection with Trestle Glen Blvd.
17.9  Paradise Beach County Park.
21.3  Road becomes Tiburon Blvd.
21.7  Join bike path on west side of Tiburon Blvd.
24.2  Bike path ends; join Greenwood Beach Rd. heading SW out of parking lot; becomes Greenwood Cove.
**25.1  Turn left on Tiburon Blvd.;** becomes E. Blithedale.
**26.8  Turn left on bikepath** and follow until joining Bridgeway; continue on Bridgeway through Sausalito to Hwy. 101.
35.4  End at the south end of the Golden Gate Bridge.

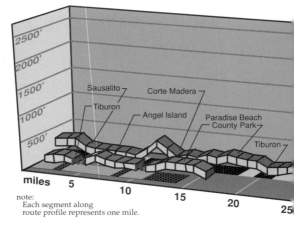

note:
Each segment along route profile represents one mile.

# ANGEL ISLAND

## 14.3 miles

| | |
|---|---|
| 0 | Start at the parking lot at Greenwood Beach Rd. and Tiburon Blvd.; head SE on the paved bike path. |
| 2.5 | Join Tiburon Blvd. |
| **3.0** | **Turn right to Ferry Terminal;** take the ferry to Angel Island; ride the Perimeter Rd. in either direction. |
| 8.0 | Return to the Angel Island Ferry Terminal; take the ferry back to the Tiburon peninsula; **turn right on Paradise Dr.** |
| 11.4 | Paradise Beach County Park. |
| **13.4** | **Turn left on Trestle Glen Blvd.** |
| **14.0** | **Turn right on Tiburon Blvd.** |
| **14.2** | **Turn left on Greenwood Beach Rd.** |
| 14.3 | End at the parking lot. |

---

### Places of Interest

**Angel Island State Park.** Picnicking, hiking, and beaches. Museum and historic sites.

**Paradise Beach County Park.** Picnicking, fishing, birdwatching.

**Richardson Bay Audubon Center.** Nature trails, interpretive displays, birdwatching, guided tours.

**Sausalito.** Small shops and restaurants. Well known as art and handcraft center.

**Tiburon.** Waterfront restaurants with views of the Bay and San Francisco.

## Route Profiles

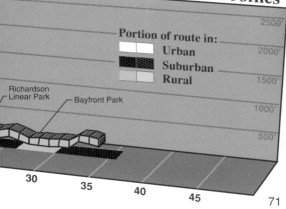

### Routes suggested by:
### David Goettler

As the owner of four bicycle stores in the Bay Area, and a resident of Marin County, David is familiar with bike routes throughout the region.    His Pacific Bicycle stores are located at 1161 Sutter in San Francisco, 2701 College in Berkeley, 2409 J St. in Sacramento, and 1040 Grant, #105 in Mountain View.

## Notes: _____

_____

_____

_____

_____

_____

# Calorie Counter

### Route: Tiburon

| Average Speed (mph) | Riding Time | Calories Expended* |
|---|---|---|
| 5 | 7 hrs. 05 mins. | 1000 |
| 10 | 3 hrs. 33 mins. | 1110 |
| 15 | 2 hrs. 22 mins. | 1410 |
| 20 | 1 hr.   47 mins. | 1930 |

### Route:  Angel Island

| Average Speed (mph) | Riding Time | Calories Expended* |
|---|---|---|
| 5 | 2 hrs. 52 mins. | 390 |
| 10 | 1 hr.   26 mins. | 430 |
| 15 | 57 mins. | 520 |
| 20 | 43 mins. | 750 |

\* Estimations from tractive-resistance calculations
  Whitt and Wilson, "Bicycling Science"

# Presidio
### and
# Golden Gate Park
### and
# Lake Merced

**A**ll three of these rides, and the connector routes between them, give you a chance to get away from the intensity of San Francisco's streets. There are a lot of opportunities to get off your bike for a picnic, or to enjoy some of the museums and attractions in the parks. If you are looking for more of a workout than a leisurely ride and sightseeing, the Presidio has a network of roads that climb over and around the headland. Lake Merced and Golden Gate Park are both relatively flat.

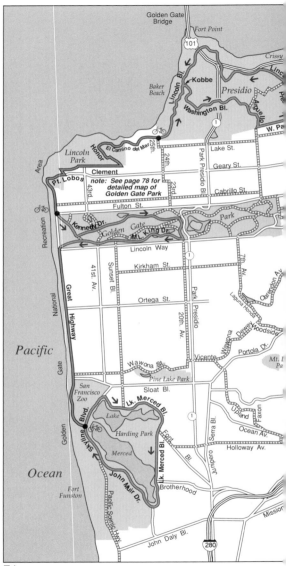

Golden Gate
Bridge
Fort Point

101

Crissy

Lincoln

Baker
Beach

**Kobbe**

*Presidio*

Lincoln Bl.

Washington Bl.

Aguello

1

W. Pa

*Lincoln
Park*

Honor

El Camino del Mar

25th

Lake St.

24th

Park Presidio Bl

Geary St.

*Area*

Pt. Lobos

Clement

*note: See page 78 for
detailed map of
Golden Gate Park*

43rd

23rd

Cabrillo St.

Fulton St.

*Recreation*

Kennedy Dr.

Golden Gate

Park

*National*

Great

Highway

Mt. King Dr.

Lincoln Way

1

7th

Av.

41st. Av.

Sunset Bl.

Kirkham St.

Ortega St.

Park Presidio

20th. Av.

Laguna Honda

Clarendon Av.

Dewey

Woodside

Wawona

Vicente

Portola Dr.

Mt. D
Pa

*Pacific*

*San
Francisco
Zoo*

Wawona St.

Pine Lake Park

Sloat Bl.

*Lake*

Lk. Merced Bl.

*Harding Park*

John Muir Dr.

*Merced*

Lk. Merced Bl.

Skyline Blvd

Serra Bl.

Junipero

Portola

Upland

Faxon

Ocean Av.

Holloway Av.

*Golden*

*Gate*

*Ocean*

*Fort
Funston*

Pacific Scenic Hwy

Brotherhood

1

Mission

John Daly Bl.

280

74

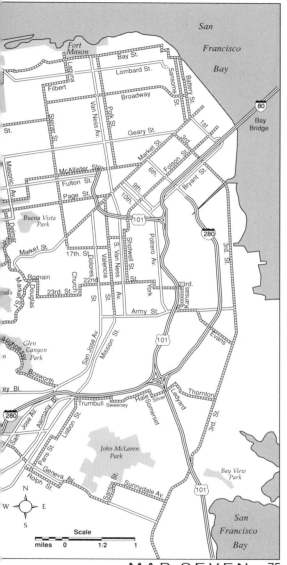

San
Francisco
Bay

Fort
Mason

Bay St.
Lombard St.
Filbert
Broadway
Laguna
Steiner St.
Van Ness Av.
Polk St.
Sansome St.
Battery St.
1st.
3rd.

80
Bay
Bridge

Masonic
St.
Geary St.
Market St.
Folson
6th.
Bryant St.
9th.
10th.

McAllister St.
Fulton St.
Page St.

Buena Vista
Park

101

280

3rd. St.

Market St.
Delmar
17th. St.
Dolores St.
S. Van Ness Av.
Shotwell St.
Valencia
Potero Av.

Romain
Douglas
Church St.
22nd
23rd. St.
York
23rd.
Kansas

eaks
Army St.

Market St.
augustine St.
n

Glen
Canyon
Park

101

Evans

Bosworth
ey Bl.

280

Jose Av.
Alemany
Lisbon St.
Trumbull
Sweeney
Hale
Silver
Somerset
Ledyard
Thornton

3rd. St.

San
Paris St.

John McLaren
Park

Bay View
Park

Geneva Av.
Ralph St.
Sunnydale Av.

101

N
W    E
S

San
Francisco
Bay

Scale
miles    0    1/2    1

MAP  SEVEN    75

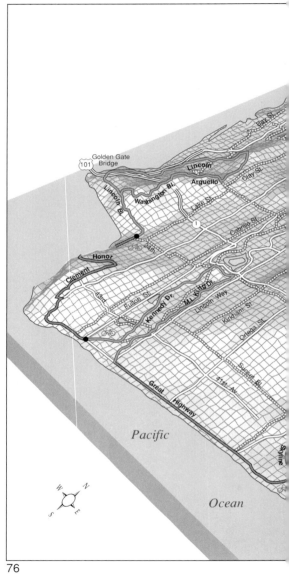

Golden Gate
Bridge

Lincoln

Arguello

Clay St.

Washington Bl.

Lake St.

Bay St.

Lincoln Bl.

Cabrillo St.

Honor

24th

Clement

43rd

Fulton St.

Kennedy Dr.

M. King Dr.

Lincoln Way

Kirkham St.

Ortega St.

Sunset Bl.

41st Av.

Great Highway

Pacific

Skyline

Ocean

N
W E
S

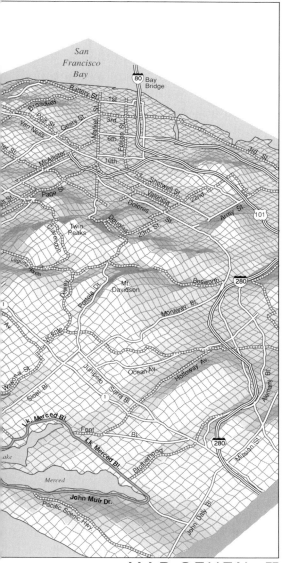

San Francisco Bay

Battery St.

Broadway

Van Ness

Polk St.

Geary St.

Market St.

1st

80 Bay Bridge

3rd St.

6th St.

Folsom

10th

McAllister

Page St.

Shotwell St.

Valencia

22nd

Dolores

3rd St.

Douglas

Clarendon

23rd St.

Army St.

101

Twin Peaks

Laguna Honda

Mt. Davidson

Bosworth

280

Oswell

Portola Dr.

Monterey Bl.

Av.

Vicente

Ocean Av.

Holloway Av.

Wawona St.

Junipero Serra Bl.

Sloat Bl.

1

Alemany Bl.

Lk. Merced Bl.

Font

Bl.

280

Mission St.

Lk. Merced Bl.

Brotherhood

ake

Merced

John Muir Dr.

Pacific Scenic Hwy.

John Daly Bl.

# PRESIDIO
## 7.6 miles

0   Start at 25th Ave. and Lincoln Blvd.; head north into the Presidio.
**1.0   Turn right on Kobbe Ave.**
**1.1   Turn right on Washington Blvd.**
**2.5   Bear right onto Arguello Blvd.**
**2.8   Turn hard left on West Pacific Ave. just before leaving the Presidio.**
**3.6   Turn left on Presidio Blvd.**
4.1   Continue straight onto Lincoln Ave.; becomes Lincoln Blvd.
6.6   Intersection with Kobbe Ave.
7.6   End at 25th Ave. and Lincoln Blvd.

# GOLDEN GATE
## 4.2 miles

0   Start at the intersection of Great Hwy. and Kennedy Dr.; head SE on Kennedy Dr.
**0.3   Turn left at the stop sign to stay on Kennedy Dr.**
**1.1   Bear right at Spreckels Lake to stay on Kennedy**
**1.9   Turn right on Transverse just before the Hwy. 1 overpass.**
2.1   Intersection with Middle Dr.
**2.3   Turn right on Martin Luther King Dr.**
3.0   Intersection with Metson Rd.
**3.8   Bear left to stay on Martin Luther King Dr.**
4.2   End at Martin Luther King Dr. and Lincoln Way.

## Golden Gate Park

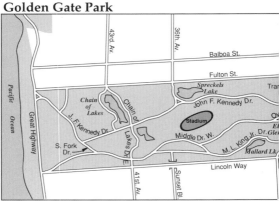

# LAKE MERCED

## 4.6 miles

0    Start at the intersection of Great Hwy. and Skyline Blvd.; head north on Skyline Blvd. or the path.
**0.5  Bear right onto Lake Merced Blvd.**
**0.9  Bear right to stay on Lake Merced Blvd.**
**3.0  Bear right onto John Muir Dr.**
**4.1  Bear right onto Skyline Blvd.**
4.6  End at Great Hwy.

---

### Places of Interest

**Golden Gate Park**
- **M.H. de Young Memorial Museum**. Art Museum and Asian Art Museum
- **Ca. Academy of Sciences**. Steinhart Aquarium, Morrison Planetarium, museum of history.
- **Japanese Tea Garden**. Traditional Japanese gardens and teahouse.
- **Children's Playground and Zoo.** Petting zoo and carousel.
- **Strybing Arboretum and Conservatory of Flowers.** Historic greenhouse with rare and exotic plants.

**Presidio**
- **Fort Point National Historic Site**. Guided tours and interesting views of the G.G. Bridge and the Bay.
- **Crissy Field**. Golden Gate Promenade along the shoreline between Fort Mason and Fort Point.
- **Baker Beach**. Hiking and fishing.

*(continued on next page)*

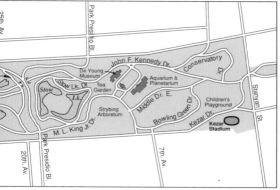

**Routes suggested by:**
**David Goettler**
As the owner of four bicycle stores in the Bay Area, and a resident of Marin County, David is familiar with bike routes throughout the region. His Pacific Bicycle stores are located at 1161 Sutter in San Francisco, 2701 College in Berkeley, 2409 J St. in Sacramento, and 1040 Grant, #105 in Mountain View.

## Connector route from Presidio to Golden Gate Park

0   Start at 25th Ave. and Lincoln Blvd.; head west on El Camino del Mar.
0.6   Enter Golden Gate National Recreation Area.
**1.0   Turn left on Legion of Honor Dr. at the Palace of the Legion of Honor.**
**1.5   Turn left on Clement St.**
**2.3   Turn left on El Camino del Mar.**
**2.4   Turn right on Point Lobos Ave.**
**3.3   Turn left on Golden Gate Park on Kennedy Dr. at the windmill.**

## Connector route from Golden Gate Park to Lake Merced

0   Start at Martin Luther King Dr. and Lincoln Way; head east on Lincoln Way, then south on Great Hwy.
*Note: depending on traffic, you may wish to ride south on the bike path in the green strip east of the highway, on La Playa.*
2.9   End at the intersection of Great Hwy. and Skyline Blvd.

---

### Places of Interest (continued)

**Lincoln Park**
 - **The California Palace of the Legion of Honor.** Art museum and great view of the city.

**Lake Merced**
 - **San Francisco Zoo**. Over a thousand birds and animals.
 - **Fort Funston**. Spectacular views over the Pacific.

# MAP EIGHT

# Briones

### and

# San Pablo Reservoir

**F**or being so close to the major East Bay cities, these routes incorporate a surprising amount of very pleasant rural countryside. While the San Pablo Reservoir loop is hard to modify, there are many possible variations to Briones. Happy Valley Rd. provides a good cut-off option, and several other alternate routes in the area are mapped. Briones Regional Park has many miles of trails for off-road cycling, some of which are mapped here. South of the park there are several towns where food and refreshment can be purchased.

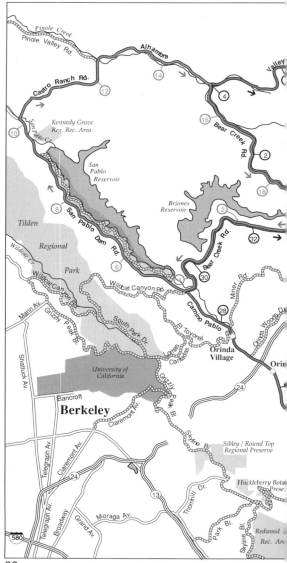

Pinole Creek

Pinole Valley Rd.

Alhambra

Valley

Castro Ranch Rd.

(14)

(12)

(4)

San Pablo C.

(16) Bear Creek Rd.

(10)

Kennedy Grove
Reg. Rec. Area

(2)

San
Pablo
Reservoir

(18)

San Pablo Dam Rd.

Briones
Reservoir

(8)

(2)

Tilden

(32)

Regional

Wildcat Cr.

Bear Creek Rd.

(6)

Park

Wildcat Canyon Rd.

(30)

Wildcat Canyon Rd.

Miner Rd.

Camino Pablo

Marin Av.

Grizzly Peak Bl.

South Park Dr.

El Toyonal

(28)

Orinda Woods Dr.

Lomas

Shattuck Av.

University of
California

Cañadas

Orinda
Village

Ori

Bancroft

Grizzly Peak Bl.

**Berkeley**

Claremont Av.

(24)

Telegraph Av.

Claremont Av.

Claremont Av.

Skyline Bl.

Sibley / Round Top
Regional Preserve

(24)

Telegraph Av.

Broadway

(13)

Thornhill Dr.

Huckleberry Botan
Prese

Grand Av.

Moraga Av.

Park Bl.

Skyline Bl.

Redwood
Rec. Are

580

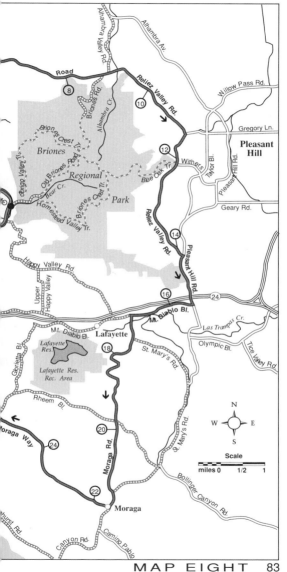

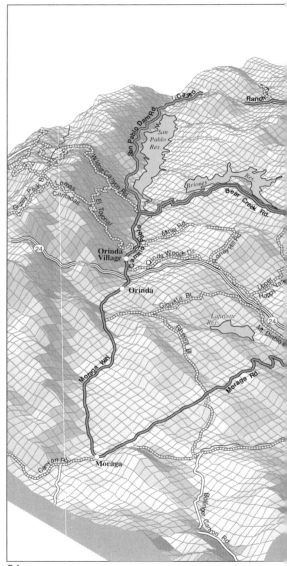

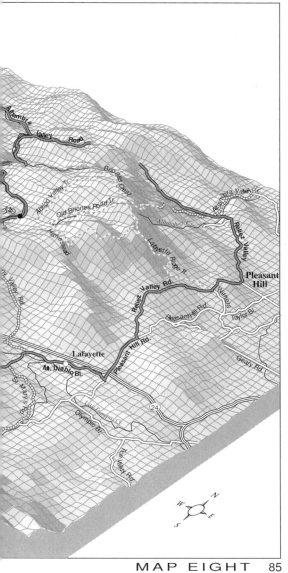

Alhambra Valley Road

Briones Crest

Abrigo Valley Tr.

Old Briones Road Tr.

Homestead

Alhambra Cr.

Alhambra Valley Rd.

Reliez Valley

Lafayette Ridge Tr.

**Pleasant Hill**

Valley Rd.

Reliez Valley Rd.

Withers

Pleasant Hill Rd.

Taylor Bl.

**Lafayette**

Mt. Diablo Bl.

Pleasant Hill Rd.

Geary Rd.

St. Mary's Rd.

Las Trampas Cr.

Olympic Bl.

24

Reliez Valley Rd.

*N*
*W* — *E*
*S*

# BRIONES
## 33.6 miles

0   Start at entrance to Briones Regional Park
(parking, toilets); head north on Bear Creek Rd.
**4.0 Turn right on Alhambra Valley Rd.**
9.0   Continue straight onto Reliez Valley Rd.
12.1 Intersection with Withers Ave.
**14.5 Turn right on Pleasant Hill Rd.**
**15.5 Turn right on Mt. Diablo Blvd.**
**16.8 Turn left on Moraga Rd.**
19.8 Intersection with Rheem Blvd.
**21.8 Turn right on Moraga Way. (food)**
**26.9 Turn right on Santa Maria Way.**
**27.0 Turn left on Orinda Way.**
**27.5 Turn right on Camino Pablo.**
27.9 Join bike path that parallels road.
**29.0 Turn right on Bear Creek Rd.**
33.6 End at entrance to Briones Regional Park.

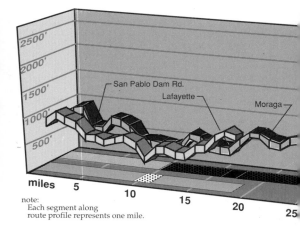

note:
Each segment along
route profile represents one mile.

# SAN PABLO RESERVOIR

## 19.2 miles

| | |
|---|---|
| 0 | Start at entrance to Briones Regional Park on Bear Creek Rd. (parking, toilets); head south. |
| 0.3 | Intersection with Happy Valley Rd. |
| **4.6** | **Turn right on San Pablo Dam Rd.** |
| **10.1** | **Turn right on Castro Ranch Rd.** |
| **12.4** | **Turn right on Alhambra Valley Rd.** |
| **15.2** | **Turn right on Bear Creek Rd.** |
| 19.2 | End at entrance to Briones Regional Park. |

---

### Places of Interest

**Briones Regional Park.** Off-road cycling, hiking, picnicking. Outstanding wildflowers in season, good bird watching, and plentiful wildlife.

**Lafayette Reservoir Recreation Area.** Bicycle and hiking trails, picnicking, boat rental and fishing.

**San Pablo Reservoir Recreation Area.** Same as Lafayette Rec. Area plus a snack bar.

**Tilden Regional Park.** Hiking, cycling, swimming and picnicking. Also a steam train, carousel, botanical garden, and visitor center.

**Kennedy Grove Regional Recreation Area.** Picnic grounds and paved bicycle trail.

---

## Route Profiles

Portion of route in:
Urban
Suburban
Rural

Orinda

2500'
2000'
1500'
1000'
500'

30    35    40    45

**Routes suggested by:**
**Matt Sharp**

Matt has been riding the backroads of the East Bay for many years. As owner of Sharp Bicycle, 2800 Hilltop Mall Rd., in Richmond, he has specialized in mountain bikes, and has become familiar with most of the opportunities for off-road cycling in the area.

## Notes:

# Calorie Counter

## Route: Briones

| Average Speed (mph) | Riding Time | Calories Expended* |
|---|---|---|
| 5 | 6 hrs. 43 mins. | 930 |
| 10 | 3 hrs. 22 mins. | 1030 |
| 15 | 2 hrs. 14 mins. | 1300 |
| 20 | 1 hr. 41 mins. | 1790 |

## Route: San Pablo Reservoir

| Average Speed (mph) | Riding Time | Calories Expended* |
|---|---|---|
| 5 | 3 hrs. 50 mins. | 520 |
| 10 | 1 hr. 55 mins. | 570 |
| 15 | 1 hr. 17 mins. | 680 |
| 20 | 58 mins. | 990 |

\* Estimations from tractive-resistance calculations
   Whitt and Wilson, "Bicycling Science"

# Wildcat Canyon

### and

# Redwood Regional Park

**B**oth of these rides start in an urban setting, climb up and over the Berkeley Hills, and venture into one of the many East Bay Regional Parks. After leaving Tilden Park, the Wildcat Canyon route makes a large loop into the lightly populated area to the east. The other route winds around Redwood Regional Park. There are many good off-road cycling trails in the parks that are mapped here, as well as a few paved bicycle trails, places to picnic, and a couple opportunities for a swim.

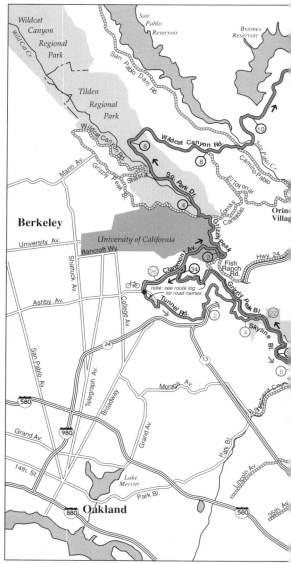

Wildcat Canyon Regional Park

Wild Cat Cr.

San Pablo Reservoir

Briones Reservoir

Tilden Regional Park

San Pablo Dam Rd.

10

Wildcat Canyon Rd.

Wildcat Canyon Rd.

6

8

Camino Pablo

San Pablo Cr.

Marin Av.

Grizzly Peak Bl.

Shasta

So. Park Dr.

4

El Toyonal

Lomas Cañadas

Orinda Village

Berkeley

University Av.

Shattuck Av.

Grizzly Peak

University of California

Bancroft Wy.

26

Claremont Av.

34

2

Fish Ranch Rd.

Hwy. 24

Grizzly Peak Bl.

22

Ashby Av.

College Av.

note: see route log for road names

Tunnel Rd.

2

Skyline Bl.

4

6

San Pablo Av.

24

Telegraph Av.

13

Moraga Av.

Broadway

Grand Av.

Park Bl.

Shepherd Cyn.

Lincoln Av.

580

980

Grand Av.

14th. St.

Lake Merritt

Park Bl.

880

Oakland

580

35th. Av.

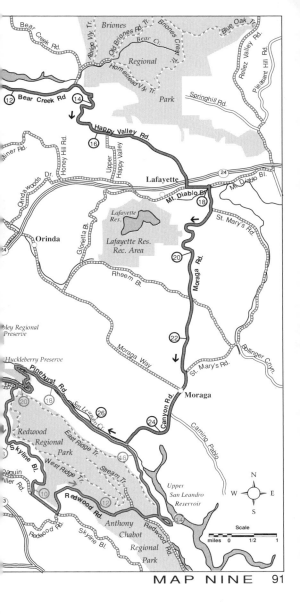

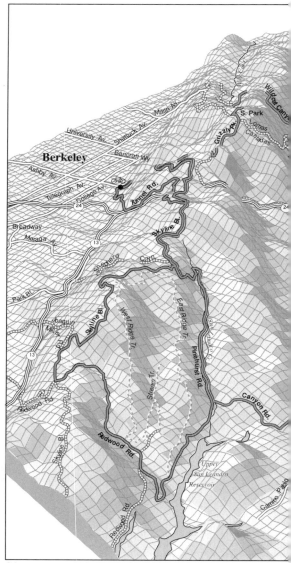

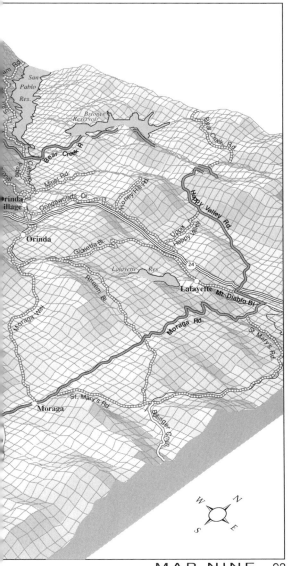

San Pablo Res.

Briones Reservoir

Bear Creek Rd.

Bear Creek Rd.

Miner Rd.

Orinda Village

Orindawoods Dr.

Honey Hill Rd.

Happy Valley Rd.

Orinda

Glorietta Bl.

Upper Happy Vall.

Lafayette Res.

24

Rheem Bl.

Lafayette

Mt. Diablo Bl.

Moraga Way

Moraga Rd.

St. Mary's Rd.

Moraga

St. Mary's Rd.

Banning Cyn.

N
W    E
S

# WILDCAT CANYON

## 35.1 miles

0   Start at Claremont Ave. and Ashby Ave.; head NE on Claremont Ave.
**2.2  Turn left on Grizzly Peak Blvd.**
**3.7  Turn right on South Park Dr.**
**5.2  Turn right on Wildcat Canyon Rd.**
6.5  Inspiration Point (viewpoint).
9.1  Intersection with Camino Pablo; continue straight onto Bear Cr. Rd.
**13.4 Turn right on Happy Valley Rd.**
16.5 Intersection with Upper Happy Valley Rd.
**17.6 Turn left on Mt. Diablo Blvd.**
**18.0 Turn right on Moraga Rd.**
21.0 Intersection with Rheem Blvd.
23.0 Intersection with Moraga Way; continue straight onto Canyon Rd. (food)
**24.9 Turn right on Pinehurst Rd.**
**28.9 Turn right on Skyline Blvd.**
29.8 Intersection with Cotton Blvd.
**30.7 Turn right on Grizzly Peak Blvd.**
**32.7 Turn left on Marlborough Ter.**
**33.0 Turn right on Norfolk Rd.; then right on Devon; then turn left on Strathmoor Dr.**
**33.3 Turn left on Drury Rd.**
**33.6 Turn left on Amito.**
**33.7 Turn right on Alvarado Rd.**
**34.1 Turn left on Claremont Ave.**
35.1 End at Ashby Ave. and Claremont Ave.

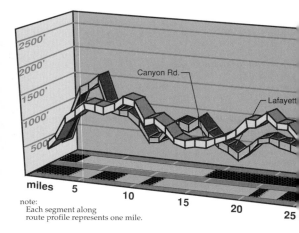

note:
Each segment along
route profile represents one mile.

# REDWOOD REGIONAL PARK

## 26.4 miles

| | |
|---|---|
| 0 | Start at Claremont Ave. and Ashby Ave.; head east on Ashby Ave. |
| **0.1** | **Turn right on Domingo Ave.** |
| | **Turn left on El Camino Real.** |
| **0.5** | **Turn left on The Uplands.** |
| **0.7** | **Turn right on Tunnel Rd.** |
| **1.2** | **Turn left to stay on Tunnel Rd.** |
| **1.5** | **Turn left to stay on Tunnel Rd.** |
| | **Turn right to stay on Tunnel Rd.** |
| 4.8 | Intersection with Grizzly Peak Blvd. |
| 6.5 | Intersection with Shepard Canyon Rd. and Pinehurst Rd. |
| 6.9 | Redwood Regional Park - Skyline Gate. |
| 10.1 | Intersection with Joaquin Miller Rd.; **turn left to stay on Skyline Blvd.** |
| **10.9** | **Turn left on Redwood Rd. (food).** |
| **13.4** | **Turn left on Pinehurst Rd.** |

(Continued on next page)

---

### Places of Interest

**Lafayette Reservoir Recreation Area.** Bicycle and hiking trails, picnicking, boat rental and fishing.
**Tilden Regional Park.** Hiking, cycling, swimming and picnicking. Also a steam train, carousel, botanic garden, and visitor center.
**Redwood Regional Park.** Hiking and off-road cycling trails. Playgrounds and picnicking.

# Route Profiles

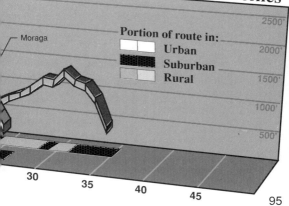

**Routes suggested by:**
**James Hill**

As a member of the Missing Link Bicycles collective, 1988 Shattuck Ave. in Berkeley, James spends a lot of time with bicycles and cyclists. He is a former bicycle messenger and does a lot of off-road riding in the East Bay region.

### Redwood Regional Park
Mileage Log (con't)

16.2 Intersection with Canyon Rd.
**20.2 Turn right on Skyline Blvd.**
21.1 Intersection with Cotton Blvd.
**22.0 Turn right on Grizzly Peak Blvd.**
**24.0 Turn left on Marlborough Ter.**
**24.3 Turn right on Norfolk Rd.; turn right on Devon; turn left on Strathmoor Dr.**
**24.6 Turn left on Drury Rd.**
**24.9 Turn left on Amito.**
**25.0 Turn right on Alvarado Rd.**
**25.4 Turn left on Claremont Ave.**
26.4 End at Ashby Ave. and Claremont Ave.

# Calorie Counter

**Route:  Wildcat Canyon**

| Average Speed (mph) | Riding Time | Calories Expended* |
|---|---|---|
| 5 | 7 hrs. 01 mins. | 1000 |
| 10 | 3 hrs. 31 mins. | 1110 |
| 15 | 2 hrs. 20 mins. | 1410 |
| 20 | 1 hr.  45 mins. | 1930 |

**Route:  Redwood Regional Park**

| Average Speed (mph) | Riding Time | Calories Expended* |
|---|---|---|
| 5 | 5 hrs. 17 mins. | 730 |
| 10 | 2 hrs. 38 mins. | 800 |
| 15 | 1 hr.  44 mins. | 950 |
| 20 | 1 hr.  18 mins. | 1390 |

* Estimations from tractive-resistance calculations
  Whitt and Wilson, "Bicycling Science"

# Around
# Mt. Diablo

### and

# Diablo Summit

**T**he summit of Mt. Diablo is 3,849 ft., but seems higher because it rises so abruptly from the surrounding countryside. If you are hardy enough to make the climb to the top, you will be rewarded with exceptional views of the Sierra, San Francisco and the Bay, Mt. Lassen, the Central Valley, and Mt. Hamilton. The climate is distinctly drier and warmer here than on the coast, so be sure to carry plenty of water with you. Once you leave the Walnut Creek area, especially on the longer route, food and water both are hard to come by.

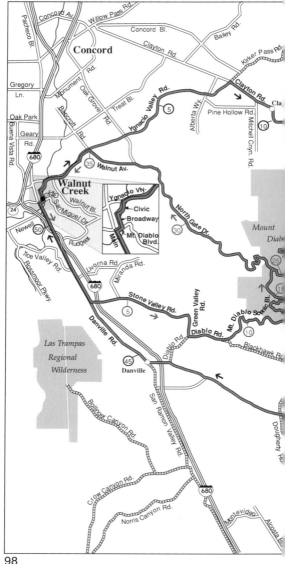

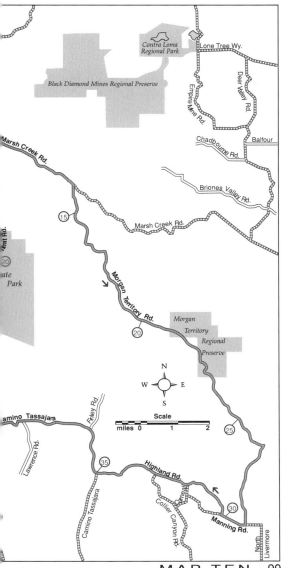

Contra Loma
Regional Park

Lone Tree Wy.

Black Diamond Mines Regional Preserve

Empire Mine Rd.

Deer Valley Rd.

Chadbourne Rd.

Balfour

Marsh Creek Rd.

Briones Valley Rd.

(15)

Marsh Creek Rd.

mit Rd.

(20)

ate
Park

Morgan Territory Rd.

(20)

Morgan
Territory
Regional
Preserve

N
W   E
S

Scale
miles 0   1   2

(25)

amino Tassajara

Finley Rd.

Lawrence Rd.

(35)

Highland Rd.

Camino Tassajara

Collier Canyon Rd.

Manning Rd.

(30)

North Livermore

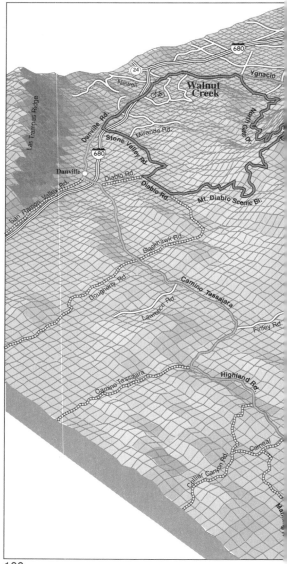

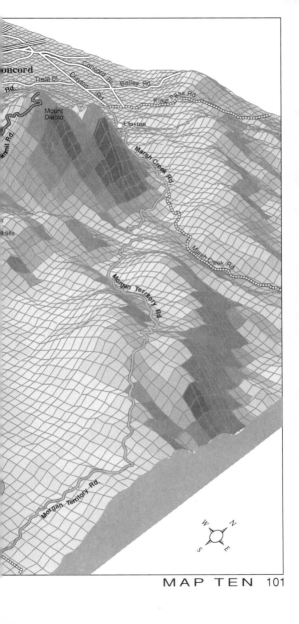

oncord

Treat Bl.

Rd.

Concord Bl.

Clayton Rd.

Bailey Rd.

Kirke Pass Rd.

Mount Diablo

Clayton

Marsh Creek Rd.

Marsh Creek Rd.

Hills

Morgan Territory Rd.

Mount Diablo

Morgan Territory Rd.

W N S E

# AROUND MT. DIABLO

## 51.2 miles

0   Start at Mt. Diablo Blvd. and Broadway in Walnut Creek; head north on Broadway.

**0.4 Turn right on Civic Dr.**

**0.7 Turn right on Ygnacio Valley Rd.**

**7.9 Turn right on Clayton Rd.**

9.3   Town of Clayton; continue through town; becomes Marsh Creek Rd.

**14.0 Turn right on Morgan Territory Rd.**

23.5   Morgan Territory Regional Preserve (parking , toilet, water).

**29.2 Turn right on Manning Rd.**

**30.1 Turn right on Highland Rd.**

32.9   Intersection with Collier Canyon Rd.

**35.0 Turn right on Camino Tassajara.**

**42.7 Turn right to stay on Camino Tassajara at intersection with Sycamore Valley Rd.**

**43.9 Turn left on Diablo Rd.**

**44.6 Turn right on Hartz Ave.;** becomes Danville Blvd.

47.4   Intersection with Stone Valley Rd.

49.6   Danville Blvd. becomes S. Main St.

**51.1 Turn right on Mt. Diablo Blvd.**

51.2   End at Broadway.

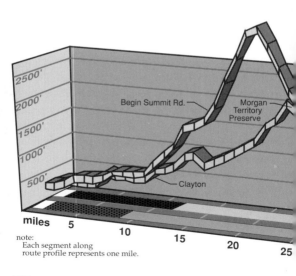

note:
Each segment along route profile represents one mile.

# DIABLO SUMMIT

## 37.4 miles

0   Start at Mt. Diablo Blvd. and Broadway in Walnut Creek; head west on Mt. Diablo Blvd.
**0.1 Turn left on Main St.**
1.6   Main St. becomes Danville Blvd.
**3.8 Turn left on Stone Valley Rd.**
6.6   Becomes Green Valley Rd.
**7.7 Turn left on Diablo Rd.**
**9.5 Bear left onto Mt. Diablo Scenic Bl. (S. Gate Rd.)**
10.5 Entrance to Mt. Diablo State Park.
**16.4 Turn right on Summit Rd.**
17.1 Oak Knoll picnic area.
**21.0 Summit of Mt. Diablo ; turn around point.**
25.6 Intersection with South Gate Rd. (Mt. Diablo Scenic Bl.); continue straight onto North Gate Dr.
**33.4 Turn left on Walnut Ave.**
**35.0 Turn left on Ygnacio Valley Rd.**
**36.7 Turn left on Civic Dr.**
**37.0 Turn left on Broadway.**
37.4 End at Mt. Diablo Blvd.

---

### Places of Interest

**Mt. Diablo State Park.** Hiking and sight-seeing. Wildflowers in a wilderness setting.
**Las Trampas Regional Wilderness.** Hiking, picnicking, outstanding vistas.
**Contra Loma Regional Park.** Swimming, picnicking, boating. Paved bicycle and walking trails.

---

# Route Profiles

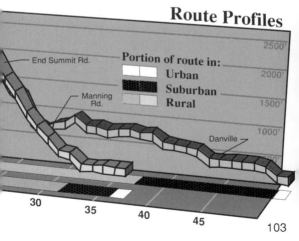

Portion of route in:
- Urban
- Suburban
- Rural

End Summit Rd.
Manning Rd.
Danville

2500'
2000'
1500'
1000'

30    35    40    45

**Routes suggested by:**
**James Hill**

As a member of the Missing Link Bicycles collective, 1988 Shattuck Ave. in Berkeley, James spends a lot of time with bicycles and cyclists. He is a former bicycle messenger and does a lot of off-road riding in the East Bay region.

**Notes:** _____

_____

_____

_____

_____

_____

# Calorie Counter

### Route: Around Mt. Diablo

| Average Speed (mph) | Riding Time | Calories Expended* |
|---|---|---|
| 5 | 10 hrs. 14 mins. | 1410 |
| 10 | 5 hrs. 7 mins. | 1550 |
| 15 | 3 hrs. 25 mins. | 1980 |
| 20 | 2 hrs. 34 mins. | 2660 |

### Route: Diablo Summit

| Average Speed (mph) | Riding Time | Calories Expended* |
|---|---|---|
| 5 | 7 hrs. 29 mins. | 1020 |
| 10 | 3 hrs. 45 mins. | 1130 |
| 15 | 2 hrs. 30 mins. | 1430 |
| 20 | 1 hr. 52 mins. | 1960 |

\* Estimations from tractive-resistance calculations
Whitt and Wilson, "Bicycling Science"

# Cañada Road

### and

# The Loop

The Loop is a relatively flat 15 mile route that is well known to Stanford University students and staff. There are several ways to extend the ride, and the choices are defined by your interest in hill climbing. Heading northwest keeps you in the lower foothills and valley, while those roads leading to Skyline Blvd. climb steeply into the Santa Cruz Mountains. Cañada Rd. provides a good warm-up before ascending to the ridgeline of the coast range. King's Mtn. Rd. is very steep and narrow and full of tight curves - exercise extra caution when coming down this hill.

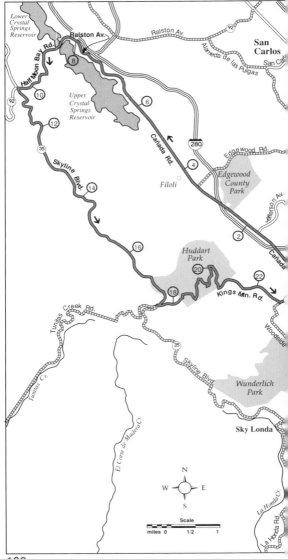

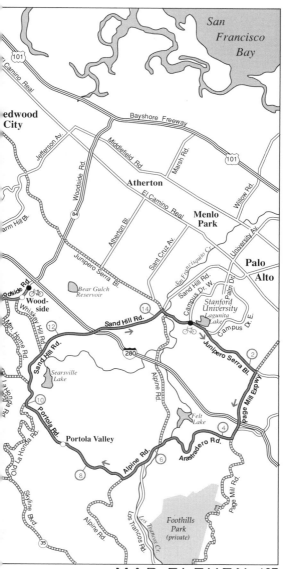

San Francisco Bay

101
El Camino Real

Bayshore Freeway

edwood City

Jefferson Av.

Woodside Rd.

Middlefield Rd.

Marsh Rd.

101

Atherton

Willow Rd.

84

arm Hill Bl.

Atherton Bl.

El Camino Real

Menlo Park

Junipero Serra Bl.

Sant Cruz Av.

University Av.

Palo Alto

oodside Rd.

San Francisquito Cr.

Woodside

Bear Gulch Reservoir

Sand Hill Rd. W.

Campus Dr. W.

Whiskey Hill Rd.

12

14

Sand Hill Rd.

Stanford University

Lagunita Lake

Campus Dr. E.

Junipero Serra Bl.

2

tn. Home Rd.

280

Page Mill Expwy.

a Honda Rd.

Sand Hill Rd.

Searsville Lake

Alpine Rd.

Felt Lake

4

10

Portola Rd.

Portola Valley

Arastradero Rd.

Old La Honda Rd.

6

Page Mill Rd.

8

Alpine Rd.

Skyline Blvd.

Alpine Rd.

Los Trancos Cr.

Foothills Park (private)

35

MAP ELEVEN 107

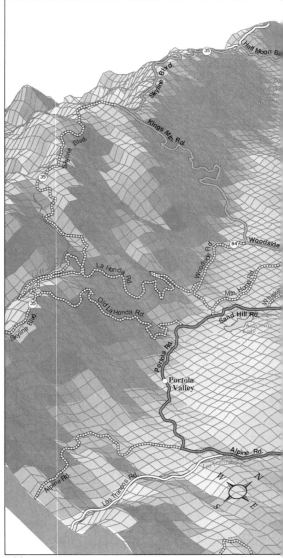

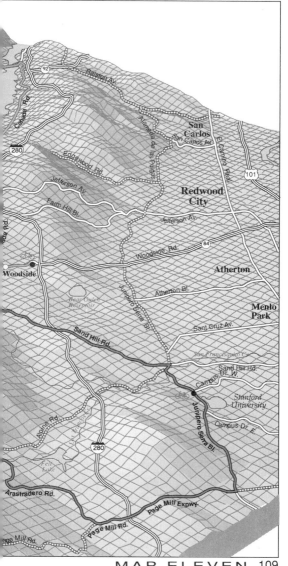

# CANADA ROAD

## 24.1 miles

- 0    Start at the Park and Ride parking lot at Woodside Rd. and I-280; head south on Woodside Rd. (Hwy 84).
- 0.5   Intersection with Whiskey Hill Rd.
- **0.7   Turn right on Cañada Road.**
  *Note: Cañada Rd. is open to "bikes only" every 1st & 3rd Sunday, April - October (from Edgewood Rd. to Hwy. 92).*
- 1.8   Intersection with Jefferson Ave.
- 3.5   Intersection with Edgewood Rd.
- **7.6   Turn left on Ralston Ave.**
- 8.2   Continue straight onto Half Moon Bay Rd. (Hwy. 92).
- **10.3 Turn left on Skyline Blvd.**
- **17.5 Turn left on Kings Mtn. Rd.**
- **22.6 Turn left on Woodside Rd. (Hwy. 84).**
- 23.4 Intersection with Cañada Rd.
- 24.1 End at I-280.

---

### Points of Interest

**Edgewood County Park.** 486 acres of open grassland and trails.

**Huddart Park.** 974 acres of hillside park with streams and canyons. Hiking and picnicking.

---

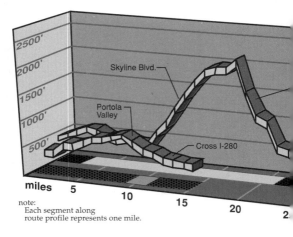

note:
Each segment along
route profile represents one mile.

# THE LOOP

## 15 miles

0  Start at Campus Dr. W. and Junipero Serra Blvd.; head east on Junipero Serra Blvd.
**2.2 Turn right on Page Mill Rd.**
**2.3 Turn right on Old Page Mill Rd.**
**3.2 Turn right on Page Mill Rd.**
**3.8 Turn right on Arastradero Rd.**
**5.9 Turn left on Alpine Rd.**
**7.1 Turn right on Portola Rd.**
8.7  Portola Valley (food).
10.0 Intersection with Old La Honda Rd.
10.5 Continue straight onto Sand Hill Rd.
11.4 Intersection with Whiskey Hill Rd.
12.7 Intersection with I-280.
**14.2 Turn right on Junipero Serra Blvd.**
**14.3 Bear left at Alpine Rd.** to stay on Junipero Serra Blvd.
15.0 End at Campus Dr. W.

---

**(continued)**

**Wunderlich Park.** Stands of redwood, oak, and madrone, plus meadows and hiking trails.

**Filoli.** Historic mansion and gardens.

**Stanford University.** Museum of Art, Memorial Church, Hoover Inst. tower, and a beautiful campus.

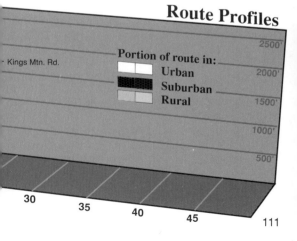

## Route Profiles

2500'

- Kings Mtn. Rd.

**Portion of route in:**

Urban   2000'

Suburban

Rural   1500'

1000'

500'

30      35      40      45      111

**Routes suggested by:
Mike Jacoubowsky**

As a former racer, and someone still addicted to bicycling, Mike has spent many hours combing the hills and lowlands of the mid- Peninsula region of the Bay Area for good places to ride. He owns Chain Reaction Bicycles, 1451 El Camino Real, in Redwood City.

Notes: _____

_____

_____

_____

_____

# Calorie Counter

### Route: Cañada Road

| Average Speed (mph) | Riding Time | Calories Expended* |
|---|---|---|
| 5 | 4 hrs. 49 mins. | 660 |
| 10 | 2 hrs. 25 mins. | 720 |
| 15 | 1 hr. 36 mins. | 870 |
| 20 | 1 hr. 12 mins. | 1260 |

### Route: The Loop

| Average Speed (mph) | Riding Time | Calories Expended* |
|---|---|---|
| 5 | 3 hrs. | 410 |
| 10 | 1 hr. 30 mins. | 450 |
| 15 | 1 hr. | 540 |
| 20 | 45 mins. | 780 |

\* Estimations from tractive-resistance calculations
Whitt and Wilson, "Bicycling Science"

# MAP TWELVE

# Tunitas Creek

### and

# Pescadero

**T**hese two rides approach the Santa Cruz Mountains from opposite sides, and on the Tunitas Creek route you can compare the slopes of each. Roads linking Skyline Blvd. to the Santa Clara Valley are steep, narrow, and composed of a series of very tight curves. Use extra caution when descending any of these roads - it's easy to go too fast to negotiate the next turn. The slopes of the west side are more gentle, especially where they follow a river drainage. Be prepared for changing climates as you cross the hill or change elevation.

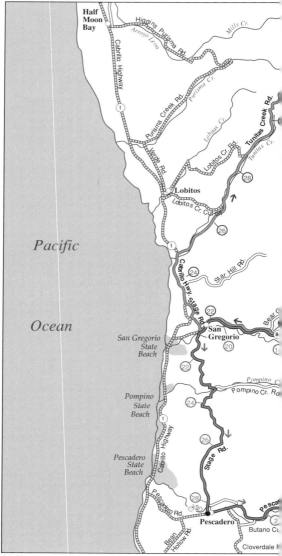

Half
Moon
Bay

Higgins Purisma Rd.

Mills Cr.

Arroyo Leon

Cabrillo Highway

Purisma Creek Rd.

Purisma Cr.

Lobitos Cr.

Tunitas Creek Rd.

Lobitos Cr. Rd.

Tunitas Cr.

Verde Rd.

28

**Lobitos**

26

Lobitos Cr. Cutoff

Pacific

1

Cabrillo Hwy. Stage Rd.

24

Star Hill Rd.

Ocean

San Gregorio
State
Beach

22

**San
Gregorio**

20

Bear C

1

22

Pompino

Pompino
State
Beach

24

Pompino Cr. Rd.

1

Cabrillo Highway

26

Stage Rd.

Pescadero
State
Beach

Pescadero Rd.

28

Pe sca

Bean
Hollow Rd.

**Pescadero**

2

Butano Cu

Cloverdale

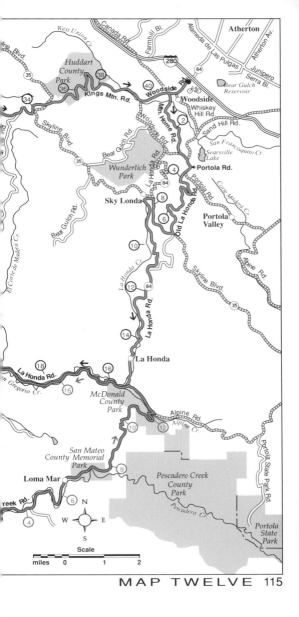

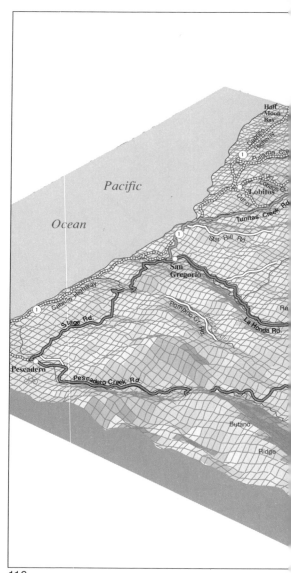

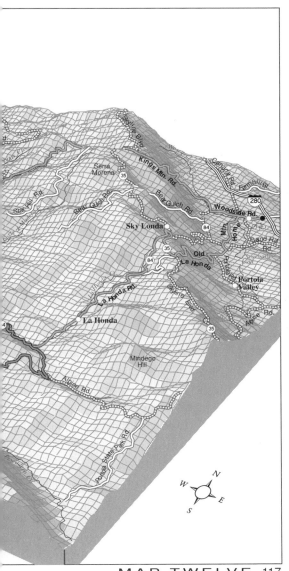

Serra
Morena
35
Kings Mtn. Rd.
Skyline Blvd.
Star Hill Rd.
Bear Gulch Rd.
Bear Gulch Rd.
Woodside Rd.
280
Sky Londa
84
Mtn. Home Rd.
35
Sand Hill Rd.
84
Old
La Honda
Portola
Valley
La Honda Rd.
Skyline Blvd.
La Honda
Alpine Rd.
35
Mindego
Hill
Alpine Rd.
Portola State Park Rd.

N
W        E
S

# TUNITAS CREEK
## 41.2 miles

0   Start at the Woodside Rd. Park & Ride (Hwy. 84)
    and I-280; head south on Woodside Rd.
0.5   Intersection with Whiskey Hill Rd.
**0.7   Turn left on Mountain Home Rd. at Roberts
    Grocery Store.**
2.7   Continue straight; becomes Portola Rd.
**2.9   Turn right at Sand Hill Rd. to stay on Portola Rd.**
**3.4   Turn right on Old La Honda Rd.**
**6.9   Turn right on Skyline Blvd.**
**8.4   Turn left on La Honda Rd. (food, toilets, phone).**
11.3   Intersection with Old La Honda Rd.
14.8   La Honda (food).
15.3   Intersection with Pescadero Cr. Rd.
**22.1   Turn right on Stage Rd. (food).**
**23.3   Turn right on Cabrillo Hwy. (Hwy. 1).**
**24.9   Turn right on Tunitas Cr. Rd.**
26.3   Intersection with Lobitos Cr. Cut-Off.
28.7   Intersection with Lobitos Cr. Rd.
34.6   Intersection with Skyline Blvd.; continue straight
    onto Kings Mtn. Rd.
**39.7   Turn left on Woodside Rd. (Hwy. 84).**
40.5   Intersection with Cañada Rd.
41.2   End at I-280.

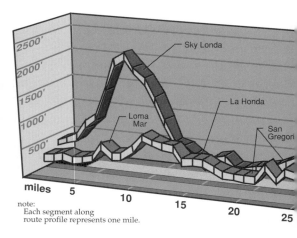

note:
Each segment along
route profile represents one mile.

# PESCADERO

## 28.2 miles

| | |
|---|---|
| 0 | Start in Pescadero at the intersection of Pescadero Rd. and Stage Rd.; head east on Pescadero Cr. Rd. |
| 0.6 | Intersection with Cloverdale Rd. |
| 6.3 | Intersection with Loma Mar Ave. (food). |
| 7.7 | San Mateo Co. Memorial Park. |
| 11.7 | Sam McDonald Park. |
| 12.2 | Intersection with Alpine Rd. |
| **13.4** | **Turn left on La Honda Rd.** |
| **20.7** | **Turn left on Stage Rd. (food).** |
| 28.2 | End in Pescadero at Pescadero Rd. |

---

### Places of Interest

**Huddart Park.** 974 acre hillside park with streams and canyons. Hiking and picnicking.

**Wunderlich Park.** Stands of redwood, oak, and madrone, plus meadows and hiking trails.

**McDonald County Park.** Redwoods and open, rolling grasslands. Hiking, views of the ocean.

**San Mateo County Memorial Park.** Hiking, swimming, camping. Visitor center and nature trail.

**San Gregorio, Pompino, Pescadero State Beaches.** Picnicking, wading, walking, sunbathing, fishing. Unsafe for swimming.

---

## Route Profiles

Skyline Blvd.

Portion of route in:
Urban
Suburban
Rural

2500'
2000'
1500'
1000'
500'

30   35   40   45

**Routes suggested by: Mike Jacoubowsky**

As a former racer, and someone still addicted to bicycling, Mike has spent hours combing the hills and lowlands of the mid-Peninsula region of the Bay Area for good places to ride. He owns Chain Reaction Bicycles, 1451 El Camino Real, in Redwood City.

## Notes:

---

## Calorie Counter

### Route: Tunitas Creek

| Average Speed (mph) | Riding Time | Calories Expended* |
|---|---|---|
| 5 | 8 hrs. 14 mins. | 1120 |
| 10 | 4 hrs. 7 mins. | 1240 |
| 15 | 2 hrs. 45 mins. | 1570 |
| 20 | 2 hrs. 4 mins. | 2150 |

### Route: Pescadero

| Average Speed (mph) | Riding Time | Calories Expended* |
|---|---|---|
| 5 | 5 hrs. 38 mins. | 780 |
| 10 | 2 hrs. 49 mins. | 840 |
| 15 | 1 hr. 53 mins. | 1000 |
| 20 | 1 hr. 25 mins. | 1460 |

\* Estimations from tractive-resistance calculations
Whitt and Wilson, "Bicycling Science"

# MAP THIRTEEN

# Skyline

### and

# Stevens Canyon

**T**hese two routes will give you a taste of both coastal mountain and valley flatland terrain. Skyline Blvd. takes you into the heart of the coast range as it climbs up to and then follows the ridgeline. Descents to the valley floor on most roads connecting to Skyline Blvd. are very steep in places, and extra caution should be exercised when negotiating the tight curves and narrow roadways. Page Mill Rd. is a good cut-off option for shortening the Skyline route. To add some interesting and fairly flat miles to Stevens Canyon, try combining it with the routes on Map Fifteen.

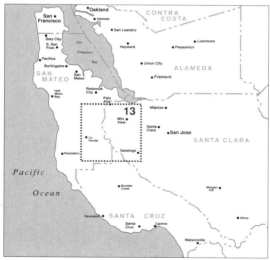

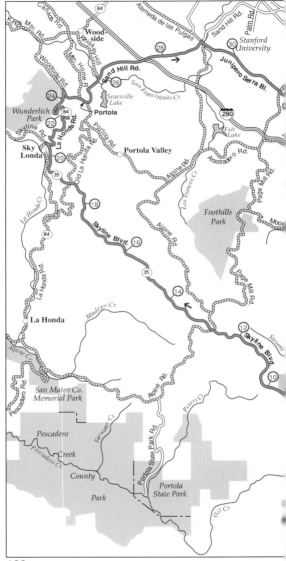

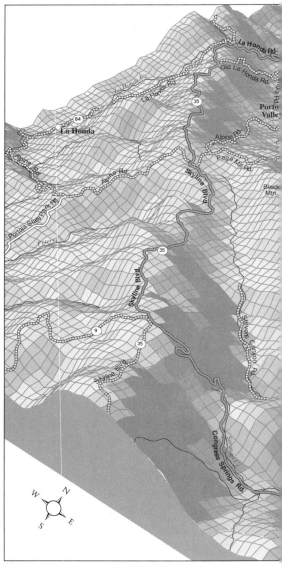

La Honda Rd.

Old La Honda Rd.

La Honda Cr.

La Honda Rd.

La Honda Rd.

35

Porto
Valle

84

La Honda

Alpine Rd.

Alpine Rd.

Page Mill Rd.

Alpine Rd.

Alpine Rd.

Skyline Blvd.

Black
Mtn.

Portola State Park Rd.

Peters Cr.

35

Skyline Blvd.

Stevens Canyon Rd.

9

35

Skyline Blvd.

Congress Springs Rd.

Saratoga Cr.

N
W        E
S

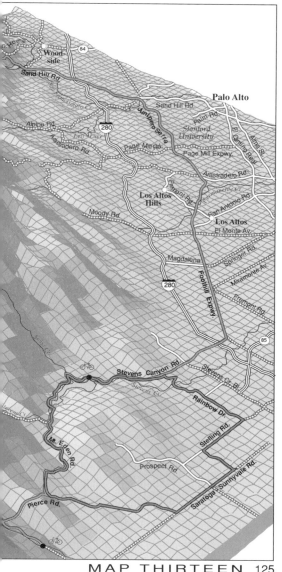

Wood-
side

84

Sand Hill Rd.

Sand Hill Rd.

Palo Alto

280

Juniper Serra

Alpine Rd.

Palm Rd.

Stanford
University

El Camino Real

Alma St.

Page Mill Rd.

Page Mill Expwy.

Alsasradero Rd.

Arastradero Rd.

Los Altos
Hills

Fremont Rd.

San Antonio Rd.

Moody Rd.

Los Altos

El Monte Av.

Magdalena

Springer Rd.

Miramonte Av.

280

Foothill Expwy.

Fremont Rd.

85

Stevens Canyon Rd.

Stevens Cr. Bl.

Rainbow Dr.

Mt. Eden Rd.

Stelling Rd.

Prospect Rd.

Saratoga-Sunnyvale Rd.

Pierce Rd.

# SKYLINE

## 46.8 miles

0    Start at the sign to Villa Montalvo Arboretum on Congess Springs Rd.; head west on Congress Springs Rd.
0.7    Intersection with Pierce Rd.
3.2    Intersection with Redwood Gulch Rd.
**6.4    Turn right on Skyline Blvd. (Hwy. 35).**
13.3    Intersection with Page Mill Rd.
14.5    Viewpoint.
19.2    Intersection with Old La Honda Rd.
**20.7    Turn right on La Honda Rd. (Hwy. 84)** (food).
**24.2    Turn right on Portola Rd.**
24.9    Intersection with Mtn. Home Rd.
**25.1    Turn left on Sand Hill Rd.**
25.9    Intersection with Whiskey Hill Rd.
27.4    Intersection with I-280.
**28.9    Turn right on Junipero Serra Blvd.**
**29.0    Bear left at Alpine Rd. to stay on Junipero Serra Bl**
31.5    Intersection with Page Mill Expwy; becomes Foothill Expwy.
38.3    Intersection with I-280.
39.2    Intersection with Stevens Creek Blvd.; becomes Stevens Canyon. Rd.
42.9    Continue straight onto Mt. Eden Rd.
**45.1    Turn right on Pierce Rd.**
**46.1    Turn left on Congress Springs Rd.**
46.8    End at the sign to Villa Montalvo Arboretum.

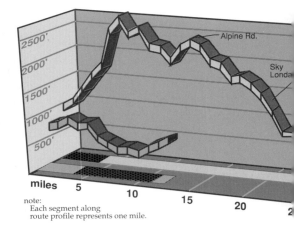

note:
  Each segment along
  route profile represents one mile.

# STEVENS CANYON

## 12.2 miles

| | |
|---|---|
| 0 | Start at the parking lot near the dam at the head of Stevens Creek Reservoir; head south on Stevens Canyon Rd. |
| 1.9 | Continue straight onto Mt. Eden Rd. |
| 4.1 | Turn left on Pierce Rd. |
| 6.0 | Turn left on Saratoga-Sunnyvale Rd. |
| 7.3 | Turn left on Rainbow Dr. |
| 8.0 | Turn right on S. Stelling Rd. |
| 9.0 | Turn left on McClellan Rd. |
| 10.8 | Turn left on S. Foothill Blvd.; becomes Stevens Canyon Rd. |
| 12.2 | End at the Stevens Canyon Reservoir dam. |

---

### Places of Interest

**Villa Montalvo County Arboretum.** 178 acres of gardens and natural forests.

**Stevens Creek County Park.** Hiking, picnicking, swimming, visitor center.

**Wunderlich Park.** Stands of redwood, oak, madrone plus meadows and hiking trails.

**Stanford University.** Museum of Art, Memorial Church, Hoover Inst. tower, and a beautiful campus.

# Route Profiles

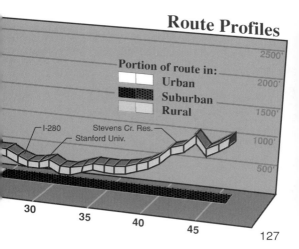

**Routes suggested by:**
**Al Knudson**

Al is the head mechanic at The Off Ramp, 2369 El Camino Real in Santa Clara. He and his wife, Kris, have explored the southern Bay Area extensively on their bikes, and have tackled some more rugged areas in the western U.S. and B.C., Canada, as well.

## Notes:

## Calorie Counter

### Route: Skyline

| Average Speed (mph) | Riding Time | Calories Expended* |
|---|---|---|
| 5 | 9 hrs. 22 mins. | 1310 |
| 10 | 4 hrs. 41 mins. | 1450 |
| 15 | 3 hrs. 7 mins. | 1850 |
| 20 | 2 hrs. 20 mins. | 2540 |

### Route: Stevens Canyon

| Average Speed (mph) | Riding Time | Calories Expended* |
|---|---|---|
| 5 | 2 hrs. 26 mins. | 340 |
| 10 | 1 hr. 13 mins. | 360 |
| 15 | 49 mins. | 440 |
| 20 | 37 mins. | 640 |

\* Estimations from tractive-resistance calculations
Whitt and Wilson, "Bicycling Science"

# Los Buellis Hills

and

# Penitencia Creek

**Y**ou will be rewarded for your marathon climb into the Los Buellis hills by the wonderful views just before you start back down to the valley. From here, the San Francisco Bay extends far to the northwest, and is framed by the green Santa Cruz Mountains to the west. The ride through Alum Rock Park along Penitencia Creek takes you through a nice blend of park and suburban settings. For a real challenge, try the road up Mt. Hamilton to Lick Observatory - all but about three miles of the 18.5 miles from Alum Rock Ave. are a fairly strenuous climb, and it is important to take along plenty of water and food.

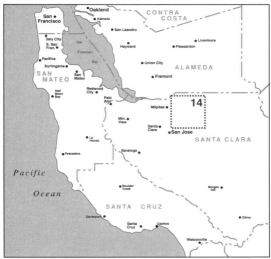

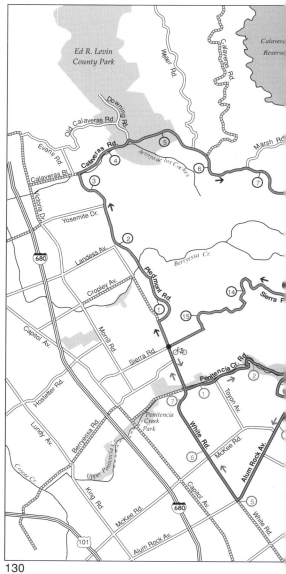

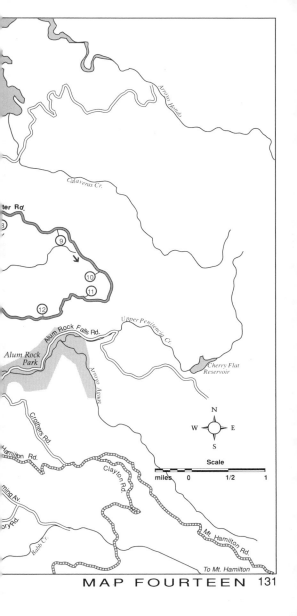

Arroyo Hondo

Calaveras Cr.

ter Rd.

③

⑨

⑩

⑪

⑫

Upper Penitencia Cr.

Alum Rock Falls Rd.

Alum Rock
Park

Cherry Flat
Reservoir

Arroyo Aguage

Crothers Rd.

N
W ← → E
S

Scale

miles   0        1/2        1

Hamilton Rd.

Clayton Rd.

ming Av.

ory Rd.

Bath Cr.

Mt. Hamilton Rd.

To Mt. Hamilton

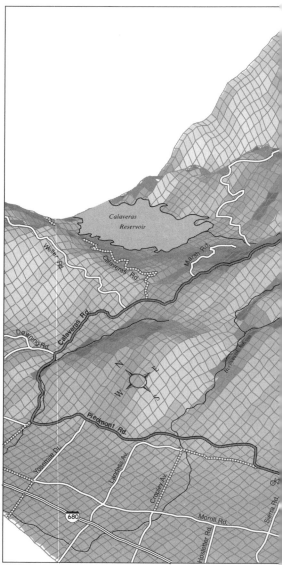

Calaveras Reservoir

Weller Rd.

Calaveras Rd.

Dawling Rd.

Calaveras Rd.

March Rd.

Browns Dr.

Piedmont Rd.

Yosemite Dr.

Landless Av.

Croyden Av.

Morrill Rd.

Hostetter Rd.

Sierra Rd.

680

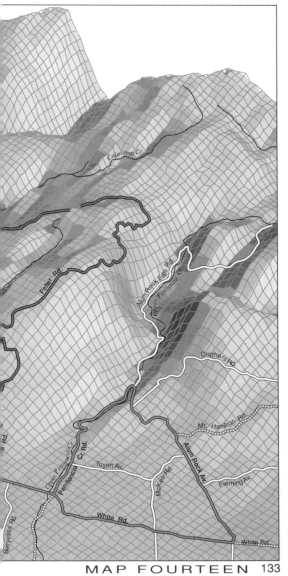

Calaveras Cr.

Feller Rd.

Alum Rock Falls Rd.

Upper Penitencia Cr.

Crothers Rd.

Mt. Hamilton Rd.

Upper Penitencia Cr. Rd.

Toyon Av.

Penitencia Cr. Rd.

McKee Rd.

Alum Rock Av.

Fleming Av.

Berryessa Rd.

White Rd.

White Rd.

# LOS BUELLIS HILLS
## 15.9 miles

| | |
|---|---|
| 0 | Start at Piedmont Rd. and Sierra Rd.; head north on Piedmont Rd. |
| **3.3** | **Turn right on Calaveras Rd.** |
| 4.8 | Ed R. Levin County Park (toilets, phone, water). |
| 5.7 | Continue straight onto Felter Rd.; becomes Sierra Rd. |
| 15.9 | End at Piedmont Rd. |

### Places of Interest

**Ed R. Levin County Park.** 1,544 acres of both developed and natural parkland. Hiking, fishing, boating and picnicking. Meadows and springtime wildflowers.

**Alum Rock Park.** Historic hot springs spa, hiking and picnicking along Upper Penitencia Creek.

**Penitencia Creek Park**. 3 mile paved trail along Penitencia Creek.

**Joseph D. Grant County Park.** (Located off the map on the way to Mt. Hamilton). Camping and an extensive network of hiking and off-road cycling trails.

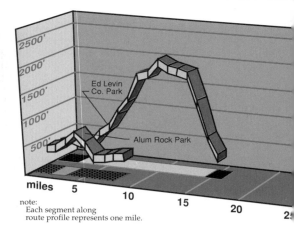

note:
Each segment along route profile represents one mile.

# PENITENCIA CREEK

## 7.8 miles

0   Start at Piedmont Rd. and Sierra Rd.; head south
    on Piedmont Rd.
**0.7 Turn left on Penitencia Cr. Rd.**
1.8 Enter Alum Rock Park.
2.8 Intersect with Alum Rock Falls Rd.; continue on
    Alum Rock Ave.
3.2 Leave park.
3.9 Intersection with Mt. Hamilton Rd.
**5.0 Turn right on N. White Rd.**
7.1 Intersection with Penitencia Cr. Rd.; continue
    straight onto Piedmont Rd.
7.8 End at Sierra Rd.

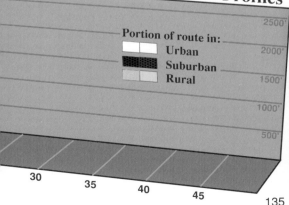

**Route Profiles**

2500'

Portion of route in:

Urban

2000'

Suburban

Rural

1500'

1000'

500'

30      35      40      45

**Routes suggested by:**
**Ken Lombardo**

Ken is the co-owner of two bike stores in the Santa Clara valley, and has developed a good base of information about rides in the southern Bay Area. His stores are Bike Lane, 1275 Piedmont Road in San Jose, and Saratoga Cyclery, 14486 Big Basin Way in Saratoga.

## Notes: _____

_____

_____

_____

_____

_____

---

# Calorie Counter

### Route: Los Buellis Hills

| Average Speed (mph) | Riding Time | Calories Expended* |
|---|---|---|
| 5 | 3 hrs. 11 mins. | 440 |
| 10 | 1 hr. 36 mins. | 470 |
| 15 | 1 hr. 4 mins. | 580 |
| 20 | 48 mins. | 840 |

### Route: Penitencia Creek

| Average Speed (mph) | Riding Time | Calories Expended* |
|---|---|---|
| 5 | 1 hr. 34 mins. | 180 |
| 10 | 47 mins. | 230 |
| 15 | 31 mins. | 300 |
| 20 | 23 mins. | 400 |

\* Estimations from tractive-resistance calculations
Whitt and Wilson, "Bicycling Science"

# Villa Montalvo

### and

# Los Gatos

**T**hese rides are among the shorter and less demanding in the book. While they don't venture into any real rural areas, they do stay in a very pleasant suburban environment. There are plenty of trees and a lush vegetation that results from a higher rainfall than found in communities only a short distance further northeast into the valley. Los Gatos and Saratoga are both good bets for finding an appropriate answer to the appetite you will develop on your ride. Either route can be easily combined with Stevens Canyon (Map Thirteen) to add on a few miles.

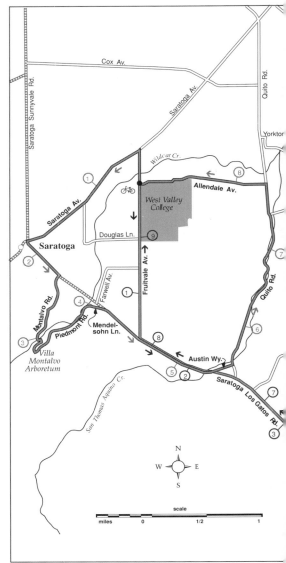

138

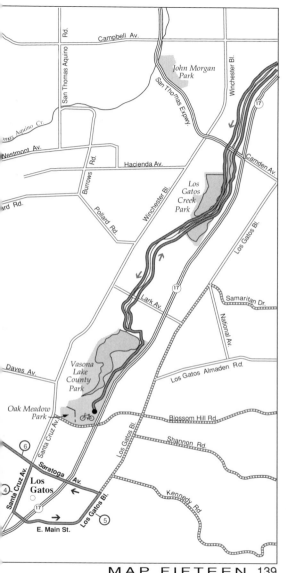

MAP FIFTEEN 139

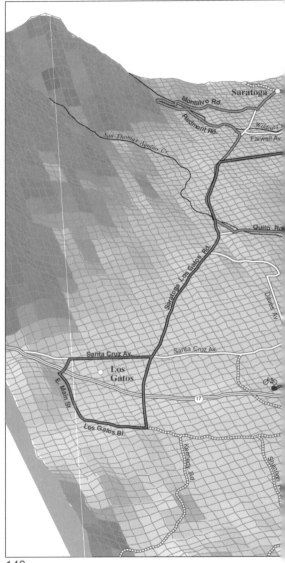

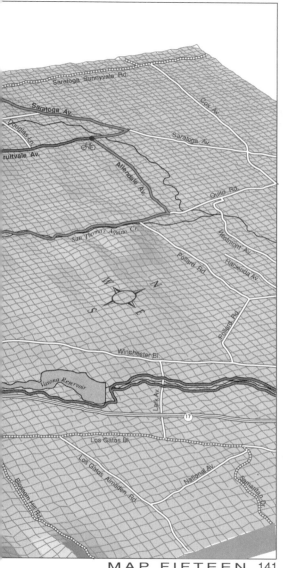

Saratoga-Sunnyvale Rd.

Cox Av.

Saratoga Av.

Douglas Ln.

Saratoga Av.

Fruitvale Av.

Allendale Av.

Quito Rd.

San Thomas Aquino Cr.

Westmont Av.

Pollard Rd.

Hacienda Av.

Pollard Rd.

Winchester Bl.

Vasona Reservoir

Lark Av.

17

Los Gatos Bl.

Los Gatos Almaden Rd.

National Av.

Samarkan Dr.

Blossom Hill Rd.

# VILLA MONTALVO
## 8.9 miles

| | |
|---|---|
| 0 | Start at Fruitvale Ave. and Allendale Ave.; head north on Fruitvale Ave. |
| **0.3** | **Turn left on Saratoga Ave.** |
| **1.7** | **Turn left on Saratoga-Los Gatos Rd.** |
| **2.1** | **Turn right on Montalvo Rd.** |
| 3.1 | Villa Montalvo Arboretum |
| 3.7 | Continue straight onto Piedmont Rd. |
| **3.9** | **Turn right on Mendelsohn Ln.** |
| **4.0** | **Turn right on Saratoga-Los Gatos Rd.** |
| 4.5 | Intersection with Fruitvale Ave. |
| **5.6** | **Turn left on Austin Way.** |
| **5.7** | **Turn left on Quito Rd.** |
| **7.7** | **Turn left on Allendale Ave.** |
| 8.9 | End at Fruitvale Ave. |

# LOS GATOS CREEK PARK

*Note: This route is mapped, but not profiled below.*

Start at Vasona Lake County Park; park entrance is off Blossom Hill Rd.
Ride north on the east bike path to Campbell Ave.
Return south on the west bike path to the Park.

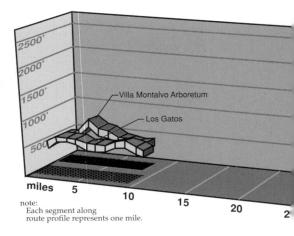

note:
Each segment along
route profile represents one mile.

# LOS GATOS

## 9.6 miles

- **)** Start at Fruitvale Ave. and Allendale Ave.; head south on Fruitvale Ave.
- **1.5** **Turn left on Saratoga-Los Gatos Rd.**
- **2.5** Intersection with Quito Rd.
- **3.7** **Turn right on Santa Cruz Ave.**
- **4.2** **Turn left on E. Main St.;** becomes Los Gatos Blvd.
- **5.2** **Turn left on Saratoga Ave.;** becomes Saratoga-Los Gatos Rd.
- **5.9** Intersection with Santa Cruz Ave.
- **8.1** **Turn right on Fruitvale Ave.**
- **9.6** End at Allendale Ave.

---

### Places of Interest

**Villa Montalvo County Arboretum.** 178 acres of gardens and natural forests.

**Los Gatos Creek Park.** Paved streamside trails for hiking and bicycling.

**Vasona Lake County Park.** Popular park for relaxing and picnicking.

**Saratoga** and **Los Gatos**. Good destinations for restaurants, cafés, and picnicking parks.

---

## Route Profiles

Portion of route in:

| | Urban |
| | Suburban |
| | Rural |

2500'
2000'
1500'
1000'
500'

30    35    40    45

**Routes suggested by:**
**Kris Knudson**

Kris is a bicycle commuter and avid cyclist. The valley and hills of the southern Bay Area have provided her with a good training ground for much more arduous riding in the more remote and mountainous areas of the western U.S. and Canada.

## Notes: _____

_____

_____

_____

_____

_____

# Calorie Counter

### Route: Villa Montalvo

| Average Speed (mph) | Riding Time | Calories Expended* |
|---|---|---|
| 5 | 1 hr. 47 mins. | 170 |
| 10 | 53 mins. | 260 |
| 15 | 36 mins. | 310 |
| 20 | 27 mins. | 450 |

### Route: Los Gatos

| Average Speed (mph) | Riding Time | Calories Expended* |
|---|---|---|
| 5 | 1 hr. 55 mins. | 190 |
| 10 | 58 mins. | 290 |
| 15 | 38 mins. | 340 |
| 20 | 29 mins. | 500 |

\* Estimations from tractive-resistance calculations
Whitt and Wilson, "Bicycling Science"

# Uvas Reservoir

### and

# Calero Reservoir

**T**hese rides, and the roads mapped as alternate routes, take you into the rolling foothills of the Santa Cruz Mountains. This is the dry side of the mountains, and much of the landscape is characterized by open grassland and shaded canyons. Several of the parks in the area are built around reservoirs, which make for good picnic spots and at least one opportunity for a swim. Morgan Hill is the only place to find food and refreshment once you leave the suburban area around the starting point, so be sure to carry enough water and food with you on the ride.

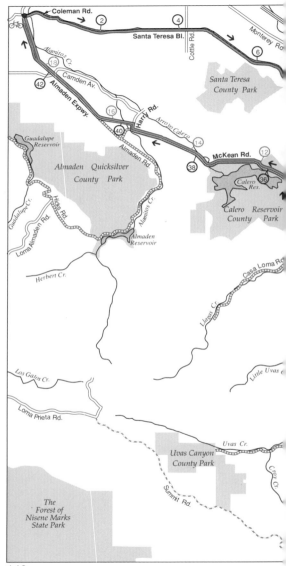

Coleman Rd.
②
④
Santa Teresa Bl.
Monterey Rd
⑥
Alamitos Cr.
⑱
Camden Av.
Cottle Rd
Santa Teresa
County Park
㊷
Almaden Expwy.
⑯
Harry Rd.
Arroyo Calero
⑭
McKean Rd.
⑫
⑩
⑧
Almaden Rd.
Guadalupe
Reservoir
Calero
Res.
㊱
Almaden   Quicksilver
County   Park
Calero   Reservoir
County   Park
Guadalupe Cr.
Hicks Rd.
Alamitos Cr.
Loma Almaden Rd.
Almaden
Reservoir
Herbert Cr.
Casa Loma Rd
Llagas Cr.
Little Uvas
Los Gatos Cr.
Loma Prieta Rd.
Uvas Cr.
Uvas Canyon
County Park
Croy Cr.
Summit Rd.
The
Forest of
Nisene Marks
State Park

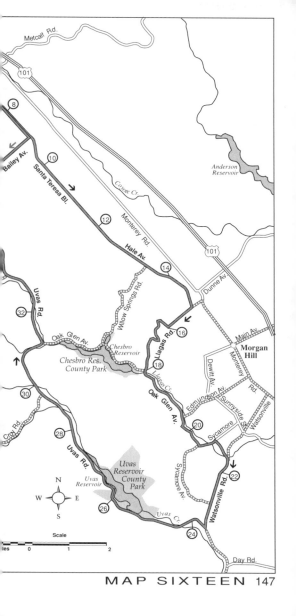

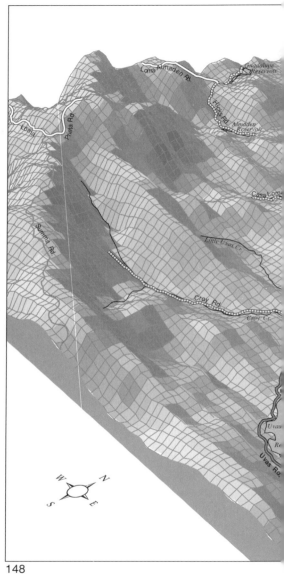

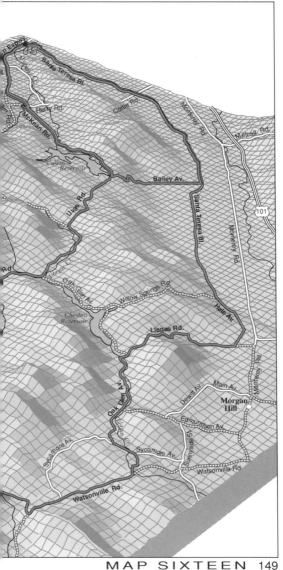

# UVAS RESERVOIR

## 43.8 miles

0   Start at Coleman Rd. and Almaden Expressway; head east on Coleman Rd.
**0.9 Turn right on Santa Teresa Blvd.**
4.1  Intersection with Cottle Rd.
9.0  Intersection with Bailey Ave.
11.2 Becomes Hale Ave.
13.5 Intersection with Willow Springs Rd.
**15.0 Turn right on Llagas Rd.**
18.0 Continue straight onto Oak Glen Ave.
**20.7 Turn left at intersection with Sycamore Ave.**
**21.0 Turn right at next intersection.**
**21.5 Turn right on Watsonville Rd.**
22.9 Intersection with Sycamore Ave.
**23.6 Turn right on Uvas Rd.**
29.4 Intersection with Croy Rd.
31.1 Intersection with Oak Glen Rd.
33.2 Intersection with Casa Loma Rd.; begin McKean Rd.
35.6 Intersection with Bailey Ave.
36.5 Calero Reservoir Park (swimming).
**39.7 Turn right on Harry Rd.**
**39.9 Turn left on Almaden Expressway.**
43.8 End at Coleman Rd.

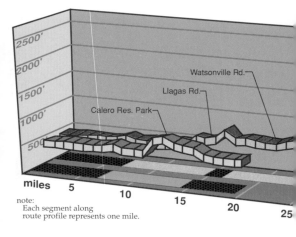

note:
Each segment along route profile represents one mile.

150

# CALERO RESERVOIR

## 19.6 miles

| | |
|---|---|
| 0 | Start at Coleman Rd. and Almaden Expressway; head east on Coleman Rd. |
| **0.9** | **Turn right on Santa Teresa Blvd.** |
| 4.1 | Intersection with Cottle Rd. |
| **9.0** | **Turn right on Bailey Ave.** |
| **11.1** | **Turn right on McKean Rd.** |
| 12.0 | Calero Reservoir Park (swimming). |
| **15.2** | **Turn right on Harry Rd.** |
| **15.4** | **Turn left on Almaden Expressway.** |
| 19.6 | End at Coleman Rd. |

### Places of Interest

**Santa Teresa County Park**. Picnicking and hiking. Views.

**Calero Reservoir County Park.** Picnicking, swimming, hiking.

**Almaden Quicksilver County Park.** Historic mining area. Hiking, picnicking, watersports.

**Uvas Canyon County Park.** Steep hillsides and waterfalls. Hiking.

## Route Profiles

Portion of route in:
Urban
Suburban
Rural

Uvas Reservoir

Calero Reservoir Park

**Routes suggested by:**
**Ken Aslin**

Ken is a former Category 3 racer who has logged many hours touring the roads of the southern Bay Area. His own ride preferences tend toward even longer, more challenging routes than those we have highlighted in this book.

## Notes:

---

# Calorie Counter

**Route: Uvas Reservoir**

| Average Speed (mph) | Riding Time | Calories Expended* |
|---|---|---|
| 5 | 8 hrs. 46 mins. | 1230 |
| 10 | 4 hrs. 23 mins. | 1360 |
| 15 | 2 hrs. 55 mins. | 1720 |
| 20 | 2 hrs. 11 mins. | 2360 |

**Route: Calero Reservoir**

| Average Speed (mph) | Riding Time | Calories Expended* |
|---|---|---|
| 5 | 3 hrs. 55 mins. | 550 |
| 10 | 1 hr. 58 mins. | 600 |
| 15 | 1hr. 18 mins. | 710 |
| 20 | 59 mins. | 1040 |

\* Estimations from tractive-resistance calculations
Whitt and Wilson, "Bicycling Science"

# Los Gatos to Soquel

### and

# Bonny Doon

**T**he Soquel route is just one of many ways to cross the hills from the Santa Clara Valley to the coast. There are many miles of good cycling roads lacing the Santa Cruz Mountains and the coastal river valleys that penetrate them. Hwy. 17 and sections of Hwy. 1 carry a lot of fast moving traffic, and are best avoided as bicycle routes. Santa Cruz is not only a great destination for a ride, but also a well located starting point for loops into the hills and along the coast.

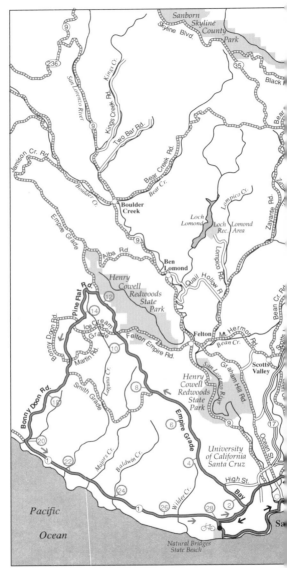

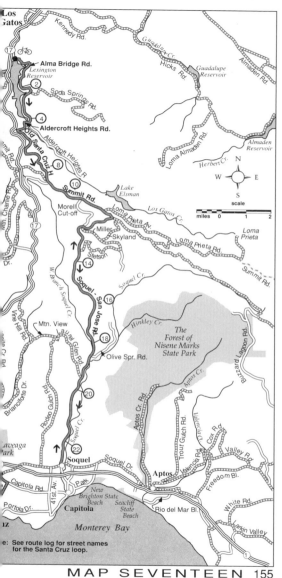

Los Gatos

Kennedy Rd.

Guadalupe Cr.

Hicks Rd.

Guadalupe Reservoir

Almaden Rd.

Alma Bridge Rd.

Lexington Reservoir

Soda Springs Rd.

Aldercroft Heights Rd.

Old Santa Cruz H.

Aldercroft Heights R.

Almaden Reservoir

Loma Almaden Rd.

Herbert Cr.

N
W    E
S

scale

miles  0    1    2

Summit Rd.

Lake Elsman

Morell Cut-off

Miller

Skyland

Loma Prieta Av.

Los Gatos Cr.

Loma Prieta Rd.

Loma Prieta

Mtn. Charlie Rd.

Stetson

Soquel - San Jose Rd.

Soquel Cr.

Summit Rd.

Vine Hill Rd.

Mtn. View

Laurel Glen Rd.

W. Branch Soquel Cr.

Hinkley Cr.

The Forest of Nisene Marks State Park

Aptos Cr.

Buzzard Lagoon Rd.

Briarcliffe Dr.

Rodeo Gulch Rd.

Olive Spr. Rd.

Aptos Cr. Rd.

Trout Gulch Rd.

Valencia Rd.

Cox Rd

Valley Rd.

Soquel Cr.

Soquel

Soquel Dr.

Aptos

Freedom Bl.

Vaeaga Park

Capitola Rd.

41st Av.

Park

New Brighton State Beach

Seacliff State Beach

Rio del Mar Bl.

White Rd.

Portola Dr.

Capitola

Monterey Bay

Larkin Valley

e: See route log for street names for the Santa Cruz loop.

MAP SEVENTEEN 155

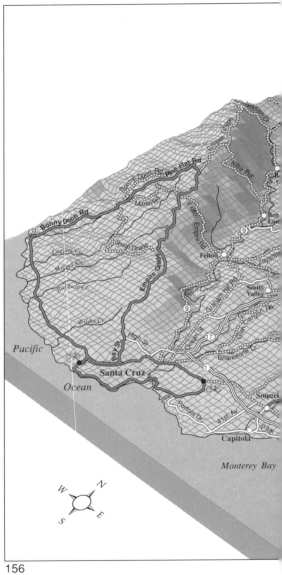

Pacific

Ocean

Santa Cruz

Bonny Doon Rd

Pine Flat Rd

Martin Rd

Smith Grade

Empire Grade

Laguna Cr.

Majors Cr.

Bull Brush Cr.

Wildes Cr.

Bay St.

High St.

Fall Creek

Empire Rd.

Felton

San Lorenzo River

Ocean St.

Graham Hill Rd

Glen Canyon Rd

Scotts Valley

Branciforte Dr.

Zayante

Ben Lomond

Alba Rd.

Empire Grade

Zayante Rd

Portola Dr.

41st Av.

Soquel

Capitola

Park

Monterey Bay

9

9

17

1

N
W   E
S

156

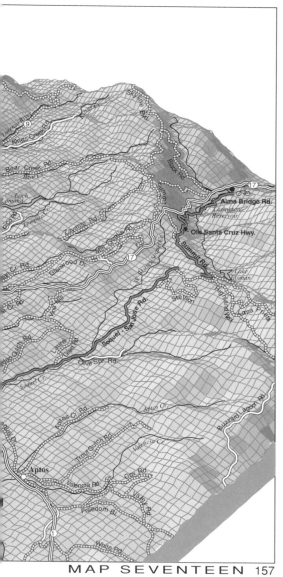

⑨ Laurel Rd.
Kings Creek Rd.
Skyline Blvd.
Bear Creek Rd.
Bear Cr.
Loch Lomond
Lompico
Zayante Rd.
Mtn. Charlie Rd.
Black Rd.
Summit Rd.
⑰ Alma Bridge Rd.
Lexington Reservoir
⭐ Old Santa Cruz Hwy.
Glenwood Dr.
⑰
W. Branch Soquel Cr.
Cr. Rd.
Vine Hill
Stetson
Lake Elsman
Highland Way
Loma Prieta
Cr. Rd.
Laurel Glen Rd.
Soquel San Jose Rd.
Olive Spr. Rd.
Soquel Cr.
Aptos Cr. Rd.
Aptos Cr.
Valencia Cr.
Buzzard Lagoon Rd.
Trout Gulch Rd.
◉ Aptos
Valencia Rd.
Cox Rd.
Valencia Rd.
Yale Rd.
Freedom Bl.
①
Valls Rd.

# LOS GATOS TO SOQUEL
## 46 miles

0    Start at the Lexington Reservoir dam; head south on Alma Bridge Rd. on the east side of the reservoir.
**4.4    Turn right on Aldercroft Hts. Rd.**
**4.9    Turn left on Old Santa Cruz Hwy.**
**8.6    Turn left on Summit Rd.**
10.1  Intersection with Morrel Cut-Off.
11.2  (food store)
**11.5 Turn right on Soquel - San Jose Rd.**
19.5  Intersection with Laurel Glen Rd. (food).
**23.0** Town of Soquel; **turn around point.**
     *Note: Return to Lexington Reservoir along same route.*
46.0 End at Lexington Reservoir Dam.

### Places of Interest

**Henry Cowell Redwoods State Park.** 4,000 acre park with redwood and Ponderosa pine stands. Hiking, swimming, fishing, camping.

**Sanborn-Skyline County Park.** Heavily wooded hillside park with second-growth redwoods and Douglas-fir stands. Hiking, walk-in camping, picnicking, and fishing. Nature trail and displays.

**Natural Bridges Beach State Park.** Surf fishing, swimming, picnicking.

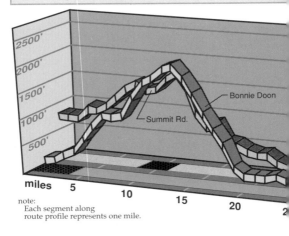

note:
Each segment along
route profile represents one mile.

# BONNY DOON

## 28.4 miles

| | |
|---|---|
| 0 | Start at Natural Bridges State Beach; head north on Natural Bridges Dr. |
| **0.4** | **Turn right on Mission St.** |
| **0.8** | **Turn left on Swift St., then right onto Hwy. 1 (Mission St.)** |
| **1.5** | **Turn left on Bay St.** |
| **2.5** | **Turn left on Empire Rd.** |
| 7.8 | Intersection with Smith Grade. |
| 10.8 | Intersection with Felton Empire Grade. |
| **12.5** | **Turn left on Pine Flat Rd.** |
| 16.6 | Intersection with Smith Grade. |
| **20.0** | **Turn left on Hwy. 1.** |
| **28.0** | **Turn right on Natural Bridges Dr.** |
| 28.4 | End at Natural Bridges State Beach. |

---

(continued)

**University of California at Santa Cruz.** Forested campus above the city.

**Santa Cruz.** Victorian architecture, beaches, amusement park, boardwalk.

**Capitola.** Historic resort town. Restaurants, galleries, crafts.

# Route Profiles

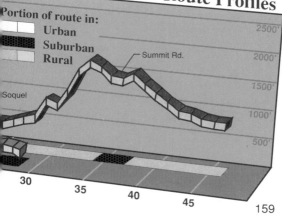

**Routes suggested by:**
**Dan Belick**

As co-owner of two stores in the southern Bay Area, Dan knows of many good cycling routes on both the east and west sides of the Santa Clara Valley. He and his partner operate Bike Lane, 1275 Piedmont Road in San Jose, and Saratoga Cyclery, 14486 Big Basin Way in Saratoga.

## SANTA CRUZ
11.2 miles

Start at Soquel Ave. and Capitola Rd.; head west on Soquel Ave.
Continue onto Water St.; across Ocean St.
**Bear left onto Mission (Hwy. 1).**
Follow Hwy. 1 to north edge of town
**Turn left on Natural Bridges Dr.**
**Turn left on Delaware Ave.**
**Turn right on Swanton Dr. to Natural Bridges State Park.**
**Turn left on W. Cliff Dr. and access bike path on ocean side.**
**Turn right on Beach St.**
**Turn left on Riverside.**
**Turn right on Eaton.**
**Turn left on 7th Ave.**
**Turn left on Capitola Rd.**
End at Soquel Ave.

# Calorie Counter

### Route: Los Gatos to Soquel

| Average Speed (mph) | Riding Time | Calories Expended* |
|---|---|---|
| 5 | 9 hrs. 12 mins. | 1260 |
| 10 | 4 hrs. 36 mins. | 1380 |
| 15 | 3 hrs. 4 mins. | 1770 |
| 20 | 2 hrs. 18 mins. | 2420 |

### Route: Bonny Doon

| Average Speed (mph) | Riding Time | Calories Expended* |
|---|---|---|
| 5 | 5 hrs. 41 mins. | 790 |
| 10 | 2 hrs. 50 mins. | 850 |
| 15 | 1 hr. 54 mins. | 1020 |
| 20 | 1 hr. 25 mins. | 1480 |

\* Estimations from tractive-resistance calculations
Whitt and Wilson, "Bicycling Science"

# Around the Bay Area

The San Francisco Bay Area is a geographically and culturally diverse area. Each of the regions described below combines a unique blend of topography, population density, and climate - and each offers a wide variety of cycling experiences.

## Marin

The combination of seaside village communities situated beneath a backdrop of extensive park lands, a large residential population, and accessibility from San Francisco draws many cyclists to Marin County's highways. It's a combination that also attracts lots of cars, especially on weekends. Shoreline Hwy., between Hwy. 101 and Stinson Beach can be disconcerting when you are worrying about both negotiating tight curves and the steady flow of traffic trying to pass you. Most of the other roads that make up these routes can accommodate both bikes and cars when due courtesy and caution are exercised by everyone.

The further north you venture in Marin County, the more rural the atmosphere. The road from Marshall to Petaluma on the Tomales Bay route is especially delightful for its great views over the bay and for its lack of traffic. Closer in, the relatively flat China Camp routes are a nice alternative to the more rigorous climbs into the Mt. Tamalpais highlands. And if you are just looking for an easy Sunday morning jaunt in search of a good cup of coffee, a pastry, and some people watching, you don't need to go any further than Sausalito and Tiburon.

## East Bay

The hills that rise behind the densely populated East Bay cities are home to several of the East Bay Regional Park System's many parks, and the roads that lead into and around these parks make for some great bicycle routes. Though not as high as the coast range, these hills offer a decent workout and some thrilling descents!

Farther east, away from the Highway 24 corridor, are many miles of rural roads that wind through rolling ranch lands and tree shaded canyons. Here, too, Regional Parks offer picnic and off-road cycling opportunities, as well as places to swim, hike, fish and just relax. Mount Diablo rises abruptly to 3,849 ft. and provides not only exceptionally fine views of the Sierra, Mt. Lassen, San Francisco and the Central Valley, but also one of the more challenging rides in this book. Be sure to carry plenty of water with you when exploring this area - it can get very hot and drinking water is not readily available.

## The City of San Francisco

The routes that are highlighted in this book for the city of San Francisco offer more of a chance to get away from the intensity of the city than a way of exploring it. The Presidio, Lincoln Park, Golden Gate Park, and Lake Merced are well known oases in the city, and are well suited for cycling. The alternate routes shown on the map will lead you through a variety of urban landscapes and offer access to almost every part of the city. Riding outside of the parks on city streets can test your nerves, and some scouting by car may be in order. Taking to the streets on the weekend is a more relaxed option, as many areas and neighborhoods are much quieter then.

# Peninsula

As in the other regions around the Bay, all along the peninsula south of San Francisco you have to go 'over the hill' (or at least up into them) to get away from the crush of city and suburban life. But once you do, there are lots of choices for good bike riding. A few major roads, such as Hwy. 92 to Half Moon Bay and Hwy. 17 to Santa Cruz, funnel traffic over to the coast, leaving most of the narrow, winding roads as good routes for cycling. Hwy. 1, running along the coast, can also be quite congested - and though it isn't the choicest of routes, it is unavoidable at times in gaining access to certain areas or completing a loop trip.

Skyline Blvd. and Summit Rd. follow the Ridge-eline of the coast range and lead you through miles of forests and farmlands. Both roads are ideal for cycling, with fewer tight curves and strenuous climbs than you will encounter on the roads that reach them from the valley floor to the east. The terrain stretching west from the ridge down to the ocean is generally less steep than that to the east. Starting a ride in Santa Cruz or Pescadero is a good alternative to making the climb from the Bay side, and you'll enjoy the rural flavor of the area.

Southeast of San Jose, out past the dense suburbs, you can put together many different routes through a gentler, more rolling and open landscape. You might try a side trip into Morgan Hill for lunch, or check out a couple of wineries near the intersection of Uvas Rd. and Watsonville Rd. Or take your swim suit along for a dip in Calero Reservoir near the end of the ride.

# Weather

There aren't many places in the world where weather conditions vary so greatly over such short distances as they do in the Bay area. On the same summer day, your selection of a ride could leave you shivering as you pedal through the fog along Shore-line Hwy. to Stinson Beach, basking in 70° sunshine on the Tiburon Peninsula, or baking at 100° as you scale Mt. Diablo.

This great range of weather conditions results from the interplay of land and sea air masses with the complex topography of the area. Ocean and bay create a marine climate in communities along the coast and around parts of the Bay - most notably in

*(continued on page 166)*

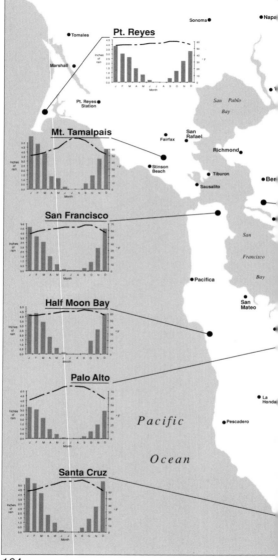

Pt. Reyes

Mt. Tamalpais

San Francisco

Half Moon Bay

Palo Alto

Pacific

Ocean

Santa Cruz

Tomales

Marshall

Pt. Reyes
Station

Fairfax

Stinson
Beach

Sonoma

Napa

San Pablo

Bay

San
Rafael

Richmond

Tiburon

Sausalito

Ber

Pacifica

San

Francisco

Bay

San
Mateo

La
Honda

Pescadero

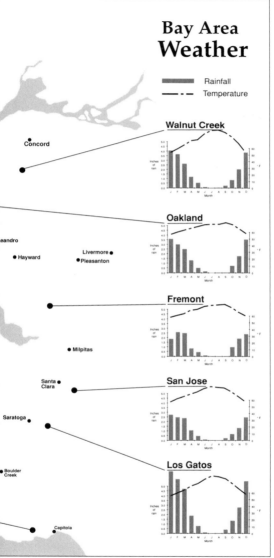

# Bay Area
# **Weather**

Rainfall

Temperature

**Walnut Creek**

**Oakland**

**Fremont**

**San Jose**

**Los Gatos**

Concord

Leandro

Hayward

Livermore

Pleasanton

Milpitas

Santa
Clara

Saratoga

Boulder
Creek

Capitola

the city of San Francisco. The effect is one of cooling in the summer and warming in the winter, resulting in a moderate year round temperature. Three mountain ranges that run north and south also greatly affect climate in the region. In general, as you move eastward over successive ranges, starting with the Marin Hills and the Santa Cruz Mountains, the marine climate yields to a more seasonally fluctuating continental climate. The gaps and passes in these ranges allow marine air, and the moisture and fog associated with it, to move easily inland in particular areas. Berkeley, situated directly across the Bay from the Golden Gate gap, regularly is bathed in the fog blown in from the coast.

The rainfall and temperature charts on the previous two pages paint only a broad picture of the region's weather. You are no doubt quite familiar with your local climate, and that usually means that you have learned to adapt to wild variations in temperature and moisture. The charts will at least give you a sense of the range of temperatures throughout the year, and the relative amount of rain each area gets. They are perhaps most useful as a tool in making comparisons, just as the route profiles are in evaluating how strenuous a ride will be when compared to one you know well.

For cyclists, the bottom line has to be "unless you're just riding around the block, be prepared for the extremes." The solution is to wear layered clothing and learn to anticipate your needs as you move into different weather at different speeds.

# Cycling Information

**B**icycle riding in the city and in the country is fun, and will be safer when common sense and basic safety rules are followed. Knowing the rules of the road, developing good riding skills, maintaining a properly equipped bicycle and matching a route to your fitness and skill level will add up to many miles of pleasurable cycle touring. Most of the following safety tips and graphics are reprinted with permission from City of Portland and City of Eugene, Oregon, publications.

## Safety tips

*In general:*
- **Be predictable.** Ride so drivers can see you and predict your movements. The rules in the driver's manual also apply to bicyclists.
- **Be alert.** Ride defensively and expect the unexpected. No matter who is at fault in an accident, the bicyclist loses.
- **Be equipped.** You will ride easier and safer if you and your bike have proper equipment.
- **Wear a helmet.**

*Country riding:*
- Ride single file and keep to the right when vehicles are approaching from behind and on sections of road with poor visibility.
- Slow down for gravel, sand, wet leaves, potholes, and other poor pavement conditions.
- Watch for dogs - dismount and place your bike between you and the dog if necessary.
- Be prepared for the air turbulence caused by fast moving vehicles or large trucks.
- Treat railroad crossings with respect. Cross perpendicular to the tracks and assure yourself that it is clear and safe before making the crossing.

*In traffic:*

There are both common-sense and legal rules to follow when you are riding your bike in traffic. The following are some basic guidelines for safe cycling.

**Obey traffic signs, signals, and laws.** Bicyclists must drive like motorists if they are to be taken seriously by motorists.

**Never ride against traffic.** Motorists are not looking for bicyclists riding against traffic on the wrong side of the road.

**Scan the road around you.** Keep your eyes roving constantly for cars, pebbles, grates etc. Learn to look back over your shoulder without swerving.

**Use a bike route.** Use bike lanes when you can. If a bike lane is not close by, keep up with traffic on narrow, busy streets, or find a quieter street.

**Do not pass on the right.** On streets without bike lanes, do not overtake an automobile when approaching an intersection or when the automobile is signalling for a turn.

**Follow lane markings.** Do not turn left from the right lane. Do not go straight in a lane marked for right turn only.

**Observe dismount signs.** Where requested, dismount and walk your bike.

168

**Choose the best way to turn left.**
Either signal, move into the left lane, and turn left, or ride straight to the far crosswalk, and walk your bike across.

**Ride in the middle of lane in slow traffic.** Get in the middle of the lane at busy intersections and when you are moving at the same speed as traffic.

**You may leave a bike lane.** When hazards or obstructions block a bike lane or you are afraid a motorist might turn across your path, you may merge into the adjacent auto lane for safety.

**Use lights at night.** The law requires a strong headlight and rear reflector or taillight at night or when visibility is poor. Wear light colored clothes with reflective tape for extra protection.

**Ride slowly on sidewalks.** Pedestrians have the right of way. By law, you must give them audible warning when you pass. (Use extra caution when crossing driveways and intersections.)

**Ride with both hands ready to brake.** Be prepared for quick stops, and in rain allow three times the normal braking distance.

**Use hand signals.** Hand signals tell motorists what you intend to do. Signal as a matter of law, of courtesy, and of self-protection.

LEFT    RIGHT

# Bicycle maintenance

Your bicycle requires periodic inspection and maintenance to keep it running reliably and safely. Several good books are available at bikeshops, bookstores, and libraries, and bicycle maintenance and repair classes are sometimes offered through the cities and schools.

Here are just a few maintenance pointers:

- Regularly lubricate your bike with the correct type of lubricant.
- Brakes should be checked and adjusted if necessary. Brake shoes should be about one-eighth inch from the rim.
- The chain should be lubricated and clean, and the gears properly adjusted.
- Tires should be fully inflated.
- The frame and attachments should be tight.
- Seat and handlebars should be adjusted correctly for you.

# Equipment

Since most of the routes in this book will lead you some distance from home, it is wise to carry at least a basic tool kit with you whenever you are on your bike. Your tool kit should include at least the following items:
- tire repair kit
- tire irons
- pump
- tube valve tool (if not part of valve cap)
- small crescent wrench
- screw driver

In addition, it may be useful to have:
- spoke wrench
- pliers
- oil
- tape
- allen wrenches
- freewheel remover

Spare parts that can come in handy include:
- cables for derailleur and brakes
- tube
- brake shoes (2)
- spokes (3)

Almost all of these tools and parts will fit into a small seat or handlebar bag, and with them you can tackle just about any problem not requiring a bicycle shop or expert attention.

# Clothing

Wearing the right clothes and being prepared for adverse weather conditions will allow you to pedal merrily through varying weather patterns. Consider including these items in your riding wardrobe:

- a hat (in addition to your helmet)
- rain jacket or cape
- rain pants
- pant leg clips
- riding gloves
- sunglasses
- thermal tights and shirt
- riding shorts
- additional layers of clothing

# Fitness

One of the most pleasant side effects of touring by cycle or by foot is, of course, the opportunity to raise your general level of fitness. It is recommended that you get a physical examination and discuss a fitness program and activity with your doctor. For the casual daytripper and serious athlete alike, exercise should not be debilitating. Pace yourself, enjoy your activity, and plan your outings to accommodate your fitness level.

*Tips:*

- Go slowly at first; be patient; and always warm up before a session and cool down afterward.

- Progress at your own rate and try to infuse a long term and consistent outlook into your activity.

- Look for variety in your exercise - both in activity and location.

- Develop a total fitness program that targets strength, aerobic capacity, and flexibility.

- Measure the amount of exercise you are getting in terms of time and intensity rather than just miles covered.

* Learn to pace yourself so that your energy resources are parceled out evenly over the course of the activity you have planned.

* Invest in clothing and equipment that matches your intensity and seriousness, and that adds to your comfort and enjoyment of the activity.

# Calorie charts

These are some very approximate figures for calculating calories burned during different types of activities.

## Walking

| Speed (mph) | Body Weight | | |
|---|---|---|---|
| | 120 lb | 160lb | 200lb |
| 2 | 3 | 4 | 4 |
| 3 | 4 | 5 | 6 |
| 4 | 5 | 6 | 8 |
| 5 | 8 | 10 | 13 |

## Running

| Pace (min/mi.) | Body Weight | | |
|---|---|---|---|
| | 120 lb | 160lb | 200lb |
| 11:30 | 7 | 10 | 12 |
| 9:00 | 10 | 14 | 18 |
| 8:00 | 11 | 15 | 19 |
| 7:00 | 12 | 16 | 21 |
| 6:00 | 14 | 18 | 23 |

## Cycling

| Speed (mph) | Calories per minute |
|---|---|
| 5 | 2 |
| 10 | 5 |
| 15 | 10 |
| 20 | 17 |

# Reader Response

The application of computer generated 3D terrain models to recreation mapping is a recent concept. In order to evaluate its effectiveness and usefulness, we would appreciate your feedback and comments. Please fill out and mail this sheet to us at the address listed on the next page. Thank you.

- Terragraphics

1. Map evaluation (circle a number):

| | very useful | | | | not useful |
|---|---|---|---|---|---|
| 3D perspective map | 1 | 2 | 3 | 4 | 5 |
| Road map | 1 | 2 | 3 | 4 | 5 |
| Route profile | 1 | 2 | 3 | 4 | 5 |
| Route log | 1 | 2 | 3 | 4 | 5 |
| Calorie counter | 1 | 2 | 3 | 4 | 5 |
| Index map | 1 | 2 | 3 | 4 | 5 |

2. Other activities you would like to have these maps for:
   hiking/camping
   cross country skiing
   driving
   other:_____

3. What other areas/locations would you like to have these maps for:

   a. _____

   b. _____

4. Of the other (non map) information in the book, what was:

   a. most useful _____

   b. least useful _____

5. Please add any other comments and evaluation that you wish to contribute on a separate sheet and include it with this response.

# Order Form

Mail to:     TERRAGRAPHICS
             P.O. Box 1025
             Eugene, OR 97440

Please send me the following.  I have enclosed a check or money order for books and shipping.

**Books:**

\_\_\_\_ copies of *Touring the San Francisco
             Bay Area by Bicycle*
             @ $10.95 each  = $_____

\_\_\_\_ copies of *Touring California's Wine
             Country by Bicycle*
(Avail, May, 1990)   @ $10.95 each  = $_____

\_\_\_\_ copies of *Touring Seattle by Bicycle*
             @  $9.95 each  = $_____

\_\_\_\_ copies of *Touring the Islands:
             Bicycling in the San Juan,
             Gulf and Vancouver Islands*
             @  $9.95 each  = $_____

**Shipping:**

$0.50 per book x \_\_\_\_ books      = $_____

             Total amount enclosed  = $_____

☐ Please send the above to:
☐ Please send a brochure to:

Name: _____

Address: _____

City: _____ State: _____

             Zip: _____